THE FASHION DESIGN BOOK

A Library of
SILHOUETTES
& STYLE DETAILS
For Drawing Flat
Fashion Sketches

STANDARD FIGURE EDITION

GINA RENEE DUNHAM

Author: Gina Renee Dunham

Chief Editors: Dianne Vogt and Wayne Vogt

Illustrator: Gina Renee Dunham

Illustrator: Sarah Marsh

Illustrator: Ariana Brolagda

Illustrator: Jazmin Perea

Illustrator: Adantia Piliang

Photographer & Videographer: Gina Renee Dunham

Video Editor: Jhonmaren Calo

Video Editor: Tetiana Zhdanova

Social Media Coordinator: Luisa Silvestre

Interior Format Designer: Shahadat A. Shakit

Book Cover Designer: Svetlana Uscumlic

ISBN: 9783952578902

Copyright © 2024 Gina Renee Dunham

Publisher: Gina Renee LLC

Switzerland

www.GinaReneeDesigns.com

Email: comments@GinaReneeDesigns.com

The Fashion Design Book

A Library of Silhouettes & Style Details for Drawing Flat Fashion Sketches

Standard Figure Edition

Disclaimer:

This book is not to be interpreted as a promise or guarantee of any outcome. The author and publisher do not guarantee your success nor are they responsible for your results.

This Book Is Dedicated to...

My husband, whose guidance has been invaluable throughout my entrepreneurial journey. Your advice, offered with kindness and insight, has propelled me forward and kept me going. With your belief in my abilities, you have encouraged me to reach new heights and embrace opportunities that came my way.

When I started my business as a side job 10 years ago, I did not know which direction I would take. Finding my way has been a relentless journey, and you have been there with me offering your support.

We moved around the world together to create a life I never would have imagined. It is better than what I ever could have dreamed. I am so thankful that we put in the work to get us here. We have gone through so many challenges that have formed us, made us stronger, and pushed us forward. I'm excited about what the future will bring.

Thank you for being by my side.

Free Supporting Sketching Videos & Bonus All-access Page
Use the QR Codes in This Book!

Throughout this book, there are QR codes that direct you to free videos. These free videos teach essential topics that will enhance your learning experience. To go to the associated video, scan the QR code with the camera on your smartphone. Most phones do not require a special app for this, but the camera settings must be turned on to scan QR codes. Check the camera settings first. Then, open the camera, tap the screen to focus on the QR code, and tap the link that pops up. This will bring you directly to the corresponding video on your smartphone.

Test your camera by scanning this code. It will bring you to the "Bonus All-access" webpage.

What is on the "Bonus All-access" Webpage?

Sign up for the FREE Exclusive Video Vault Access, where new drawing and rendering videos will continually be added. You will learn how to use this book most beneficially with new videos posted in the Free Video Vault.

Access the instant library of linked videos through the QR codes in this book and download free bonus pdfs.

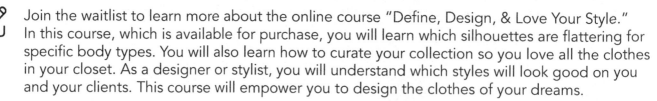

Join the waitlist to learn more about the online course "Define, Design, & Love Your Style." In this course, which is available for purchase, you will learn which silhouettes are flattering for specific body types. You will also learn how to curate your collection so you love all the clothes in your closet. As a designer or stylist, you will understand which styles will look good on you and your clients. This course will empower you to design the clothes of your dreams.

Scan the QR code here to access the Bonus page:

https://www.TheFashionDesignBook.com/bonus-page/

Try out your camera and go to the "Bonus All-access" webpage now!

Table of Contents

Table of Contents

I ENJOY *Creativity*.

REALIZE HOW *Talented* I AM.

VALUE MY *Unique* CREATIONS.

AM *Proud* OF MY SEWING & DESIGNING SKILLS.

CAN PASS ON SEWING *Knowledge* TO OTHERS.

CAN KEEP *Hand-Crafted* ITEMS FOR GENERATIONS.

Gina Renee

PROMOTES THE ARTS OF SEWING & DESIGNING TO CREATE A MORE SUSTAINABLE AND CREATIVE WORLD.

Introduction

At a young age, I loved creating. It amazes me how one spark of an idea can turn nothing into something. There are endless possibilities. I began sewing when I was young, and little did I know that this hobby would take me on an unbelievable journey that would result in a life I never imagined.

At 16, I discovered the Fashion Institute of Technology (FIT) in New York City, far from my Colorado hometown. At the time, the internet was not as developed, making it difficult to research how to create a winning portfolio to gain entry into the school, especially when it came to drawing. I found it challenging to capture the human form and struggled with proportions.

While some people have a pure talent for drawing the human figure, I certainly did not. Since this was not my God-given talent, I would need to treat drawing like a skill and develop it through practice and time.

Despite the lack of resources, I poured myself into perfecting my portfolio. I spent countless hours studying and learning how to draw the human form. Getting into FIT's fashion design program would be no easy feat, but I was determined to make it happen.

Introduction (Continued)

Through hard work and dedication, I finally felt confident to submit my portfolio. Each piece represented countless hours of effort, and I was proud of my accomplishments. I loved sewing clothes and wanted to create and design for the rest of my life.

When I received the news that I had been accepted into the fashion design program at FIT, it was a dream come true. This was the first step in a career that has spanned two decades and has taken me around the world. I have had the opportunity to work with multi-million-dollar clothing brands. My work has graced the front pages of newspapers, been published in magazines, and been worn by top gold and silver medal athletes from around the world.

Through this book, I want to share some key findings from the portfolio creation process and my 20 years of garment industry experience. I created this mix-and-match library of silhouettes and style details to make sketching easier. The library of sketches offers a starting point that speeds up the design process so an artist does not have to start from scratch.

To draw various designs to create the content of this book, I commissioned four artists. I also drew many of the sketches, updated every drawing for accuracy, and directed the entire project. I deliberately sought each artist from a different country, so various styling options are included, and five cultures are represented. The drawing and curating process took 2 ½ years and thousands of hours. Many of the drawings and styles did not make the cut.

Whether designing for yourself, a client, a portfolio, or a fashion company, drawing a garment sketch should occur before sewing and creating garments. If you do not sketch your garments and visualize them on paper, there is a higher chance that the item will not turn out as you envisioned. Sketching your ideas on paper greatly helps the design process. It is much easier to change something on a sketch if you do not like it than to change it on a physical garment after it has been cut in fabric and sewn. If drawing is not your strong suit, do not worry. This skill can be learned and developed over time through consistent practice.

Here are some of the design practicing methods I have consistently used:

✪ While studying at FIT, I went to cafes weekly to practice sketching. I set a one-hour alarm and would sketch until it rang. I call this a design sprint. Try it out!

✪ While attending fashion school, I took several art classes. Besides learning to draw clothes, I also took courses drawing live models. This helped me understand body proportions and unique shapes. It also helped me complete a sketch under a deadline because only a short time span was given. When the class was done, the sketch was done. The process forces an artist to say, "It's done," which can be very hard sometimes. It is an excellent way to learn and grow.

✪ After graduating, I had a Friday ritual: I went to clothing stores with my sketchbook always tucked away in my purse. As I window shopped or browsed the store, I would gather any design details I loved and think of any variations I would make to the designs. When I left the store or while I was

in the dressing room, I quickly pulled out my sketchbook to draw my new ideas. Through this process, I improved both my drawing and design skills.

✪ While working in the clothing industry, drawing and reviewing flat garment sketches in Adobe® Illustrator® is a daily habit. The flat sketches help patternmakers and designers visualize the garments' accurate proportions. The sketches allow product developers to understand workmanship and sewing details, and they give designers quick methods of changing colors to see how the garments can transform into different colorways.

✪ Consistency is key! The more you practice, the better you get. Think about when you started writing as a child. The handwriting of children improves only through practice and learning about spacial awareness. This same concept can be applied to sketching and learning proportions through consistent practice.

Introduction (Continued)

Practicing builds your confidence to sketch your ideas. The sketch helps you envision the item before it is brought to life.

This book will help you strengthen your drawing skills as you practice. Scan the QR codes and watch the free videos for the full learning experience.

Even with a lot of practice, drawing the human form does not come naturally to me. It is something I had to work hard to learn. My talent is in the technical part of creating garments and patternmaking, which is quite different from fashion illustration. This technical part of me is why I prefer drawing flat garment sketches over fashion illustration sketches.

Looking back on my journey, I am amazed at how far I have come. My story, which I will continue to share throughout this book, proves that so much is possible with determination and hard work. It all started with a spark of an idea that turned into a dream.

I define a dream as the vision for where you want to be in the future. For me, it was to be my own designer.

What is your dream in relation to fashion? Define your vision here:

_____

_____

_____

_____

_____

_____

If your dream still needs to be defined, start with an idea and write that down. You must start somewhere. If you do not know where you want to go, how will you ever get there?

Then, break that vision down into baby steps. These baby steps are goals that help you reach that dream.

What are some steps you can take to help you reach that dream?

_____

_____

_____

_____

_____

_____

Let's work toward that dream throughout this book.

The Medium

When I was creating my application portfolio for FIT, I did not know how to draw very well or which medium would be best for my portfolio (colored pencils, paints, etc.). There was no option to search online for this because there was little information online. I did not know markers were a drawing medium used in professional artwork.

I could not find "how-to-draw" fashion illustration books in my local library. In fact, one of the main reasons I wanted to go to fashion school was to learn how to sketch, yet I had to draw well enough to get accepted!

Without guidance, I really struggled in the sketching process. I ended up using water-soluble colored pencils. Dipping these colored pencils in water allows the colors to blend fairly well. I tried multiple types of art paper to find the best paper for that medium. The paper quality makes a huge difference in how the medium works with the absorbency of the water. However, I would not recommend water-soluble colored pencils because there is a better medium.

Later when I attended fashion school, I discovered that art markers on marker paper are a better medium. Art markers blend beautifully on marker paper. The colors can be layered to create realistic fabrics and skin tones. For the best results, use this book with tracing paper, pencils, thin marker paper, and art markers.

Except for the few extra blank pages to add to your library, this is not a sketchbook where you draw your designs inside the book.

There are two methods of using this book:

1) As a template for tracing;

2) As a reference to see how to draw the designs.

If you are a beginner, the tracing method is beneficial until you understand the proportions. Use this book in conjunction with tracing paper or thin marker paper for this method. Place the tracing or marker paper on the style details and silhouettes to draw your designs. As you become more advanced, you will likely move onto the second method of simply referencing the sketches as needed and draw without tracing.

Scan this QR code to watch a free video about the recommended tools and supplies for drawing and rendering with this book:

Tracing paper and a pencil are the minimum required supplies to use this book effectively.

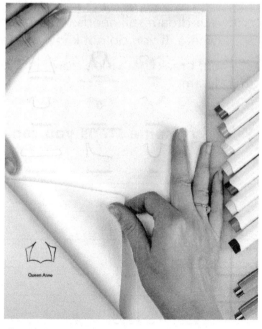

If you plan to render your sketches with color, use this book with thin marker paper and art markers for the best results. My recommended paper weight is 70 g/m^2 (18 lb) because it is partially transparent, allowing you to see the book images underneath.

Requirements in a Portfolio

Your portfolio needs these requirements to get accepted into a fashion design program:

- ✪ Inspiration
- ✪ A fashion illustration
- ✪ Flat sketches
- ✪ Fabric swatch(es)

All of these items are attached to an artboard, which is often cardstock paper. Multiple artboards create the portfolio. Some schools may have additional requirements briefed in the application process.

After working 20 years in the garment industry, I know much more about these topics than I did when I was trying to get accepted into FIT. I will share more details about each of these required portfolio items.

There are two types of portfolios: 1) an application portfolio submitted for school

acceptance and 2) a professional design portfolio submitted for garment industry jobs.

The application portfolio is not as refined as a professional design portfolio simply because the designer preparing it does not have as much experience and training in the creation process.

The following process is also used to create a professional design portfolio in the garment industry. However, many portfolios have gone fully digital, and all sketching can be done on a computer. High fashion is sometimes less digital than mainstream or sportswear brands.

If you are not using this book for a portfolio but instead for your personal sketchbook, you may follow the same process explained in this book.

Scan this QR code to watch a free video to learn how to avoid the most common mistakes in fashion portfolios:

Inspiration

The inspiration in a portfolio should be in the background or around the fashion illustration, flat sketch, and fabric swatches. The inspiration is what guides you in the design process. It could be colors, scenery, magazine clippings, shapes, or anything that inspires you in the design process to create that specific style.

Many designers create entire inspiration boards, also called mood boards, which drive the design process in that direction.

Whether you are designing for yourself, a client, or a fashion company, starting from inspiration can help make your collection

cohesive because the styles speak the same design language.

Designers in the garment industry always showcase their inspiration at the beginning of important cross-functional design meetings.

The inspiration is the story behind the creation of the collection. It will be carried throughout the marketing and sales processes to help sell the collection.

Scan this QR code to watch this free video to learn more about how to get inspiration for your designs:

Fashion Illustrations

A fashion illustration is a 3-dimensional-looking sketch with the garments drawn on a model, usually striking a fashionable pose or with a runway walk. The model is called a croquis [krō-kē'], a French word meaning "sketch." A croquis for fashion illustration is often elongated to look taller than the average person.

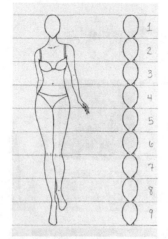

The elongation of the body is determined by the height of the head on the croquis. A 9-head croquis means that the croquis is 9 heads tall. A typical fashion illustration can range anywhere from 9-11 heads tall.

A fashion illustration is generally rendered, meaning it has been colored or shaded with

The image above is a 9-head fashion illustration croquis.

art markers. If it has been drawn digitally, then it is rendered with the software. During the rendering process, lighter and darker shades create the dimension.

The fabrics in a fashion illustration will have many folds and wrinkles, making the fashion illustration appear 3-dimensional and realistic. The sketches show styling, indicating how the garment is worn.

The image to the right is a rendered fashion illustration.

Scan this QR code to watch this free video to learn about fashion illustration essentials:

Scan this QR code to watch this free video to make a fashion illustration croquis from the standard croquis in this book:

Flat Sketches

This book contains flat garment sketches. A flat sketch is a 2-dimensional visual of how the garment looks from an overhead perspective when it is flat on a table. Flat sketches may also be called "fashion flats," "technical flats," or "flats."

An example of a flat garment lying on the table and the corresponding flat sketch.

Flat sketches are not as elongated as fashion illustrations. A croquis used for flat sketches is typically between 7 and 8 heads tall, which is the average human height. This croquis is not as tall as the fashion illustration croquis because it is meant to guide the patternmaking and sewing processes. It gives a more accurate

representation of the person's body proportions. Therefore, it looks more accurate in the design proportions. The flat sketch croquis in this book is 7 ½ heads tall.

Scan this QR code to watch this video to learn more about a 7-8 head croquis and flat garment sketches:

The image above is a flat sketch croquis.

Flat sketches often show more of the details of the garment, including topstitching, zippers, buttons, and other notions or design details. These details help the designer envision the style and plan the sewing process.

Flat Sketches: Styling and Rendering

Flat Sketches: Styling for Portfolios & Garment Industry Use

Flat sketches showcase entire garments in an outfit. The sketches do not show styling which is how the garment is worn. For example, if there is a blouse and a pair of pants in an outfit, the entire blouse, and the entire pants are drawn. There are no styling features like tucking the blouse into the pants or allowing the blouse to cover the pants. Both garments are clearly visible and separate.

Having all the items within an outfit drawn separately allows the designer to mix and match the items to create a cohesive collection. This process is referred to as merchandising and is an integral step in the design process.

Scan this QR code to watch this free video to learn how to draw a flat garment sketch with *The Fashion Design Book*:

Flat Sketches: Styling for Personal Use

When drawing flat sketches for your personal use, drawing each item separately is not required, although it may help you create a cohesive collection since separates are easy to mix and match.

As an additional step, you may combine garments to create complete outfits. Style them for how you wear them, such as tucking in items, folding cuffs, and layering items. This styling process helps envision how to wear the articles and create outfits.

Scan this QR code to watch this free video to learn more about styling for flat sketches:

Flat Sketches: Rendering for Portfolios & Personal Use

Flat sketches are often black and white in portfolios, but some designers render them with markers. If you are creating an acceptance portfolio for a school, check the briefing to see if the flat sketches should be black and white or colored. If the briefing does not list a requirement or if it is for a professional portfolio, keep the flat sketch a line drawing and do not render it.

Even though portfolio and garment industry technical sketches do not require flat sketches to be rendered, the rendering process can help the designer visualize the style. To render, I recommend using art markers and thin marker paper. However, use the medium of your choice.

For personal use, render your flat sketches with markers to envision the style accurately.

A flat sketch tends to show fewer wrinkles in the fabric because it is 2-dimensional. Therefore, if the flat sketch is rendered, it looks flatter than a fashion illustration.

During the rendering process, layer many tones to achieve a more realistic and 3-dimensional result. Generally, white and high-contrast tones create highlights and represent a shinier fabric. Matte fabric tends to have highlights with more tonal colors.

Scan this QR code to watch this free video to learn the best techniques in rendering with markers and practice your skills:

To sign up for the Free Video Vault, where I add rendering videos as I create them, scan this QR code:

Flat Sketches for the Garment Industry

Flat sketches for the garment industry are used in two ways: technical and visual.

Flat Sketches for the Garment Industry – Technical Usage

The flat sketch for technical usage guides the product development process. It is a communication tool for the patternmakers, developers, technical designers, and factories about how the garment should be constructed. For these purposes there are often many features highlighted with text and arrows pointing to specific parts of the garment, including the types of topstitching, zippers, buttons, and other notions or design features. These features are referred to as technical details.

The document with the flat sketch and technical details may be called a garment sketch, technical sketch, or tech-pack sketch. Every brand has its name for this document.

Generally, flat sketches for the factories are black and white so all the details are clearly visible. If something is detailed on the garment, there is often a close-up sketch of that design feature. Measurements specific to the design are often included.

The document with the flat sketch and technical details is used for the factories' quality control lines, so all the information must be accurate. This flat drawing is entirely digitally sketched, generally in Adobe® Illustrator® or in 3D design software.

Scan this QR code to watch a free video about the importance of technical flat garment sketches in the fashion industry:

Scan this QR code to watch a free video about the role of technical flat garment sketches throughout the product creation cycle:

An Example of a Technical Flat Garment Sketch Created with Adobe® Illustrator®

Company Logo   Company Name   Style Number: Style Name: Season
                                                     Style Description: A-line Overblouse with a Loose Fit   Year

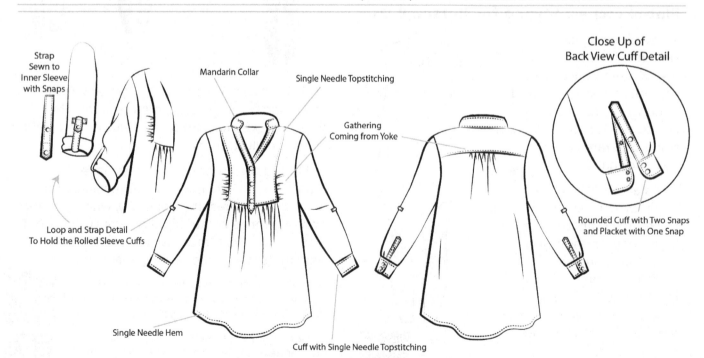

Strap Sewn to Inner Sleeve with Snaps

Mandarin Collar

Single Needle Topstitching

Gathering Coming from Yoke

Close Up of Back View Cuff Detail

Loop and Strap Detail To Hold the Rolled Sleeve Cuffs

Rounded Cuff with Two Snaps and Placket with One Snap

Single Needle Hem

Cuff with Single Needle Topstitching

Flat Sketches for the Garment Industry

Flat Sketches for the Garment Industry – Visual Usage

The same flat sketch but without the technical details is used for visual purposes throughout the product development cycle, including in merchandising, sales, design, and product creation team meetings.

Flat sketches are often black and white for initial design and product creation meetings, though this varies across brands. Rendering often takes place later in the product creation cycle. The colored images are then shown to wider teams like sales and marketing. Rendering is most commonly done on the computer in Adobe® Illustrator® or 3D design software.

Merchandising, sales, and marketing departments mix and match the rendered styles to review the collection. Flat sketches may also be used in product books for the sales teams to sell the garments to retail store buyers.

Since many other departments use these images, flat garment sketches are often not overly technical in appearance. Some slight wrinkles in the fabric and rendering shading add a more realistic look. This helps the sales teams, buyers, and marketing teams to visualize the styles. Proportions may not be entirely to scale for flat sketches because the designer must also make the garment look visually appealing for these other departments. Every clothing company has different requirements for flat garment sketches based on the teams that utilize the images. When the drawings are too flat, overly technical, or completely proportional, sometimes the visual appearance is not well-received by other teams or buyers. The sketches in this book strive toward a visually-appealing direction in appearance for this reason.

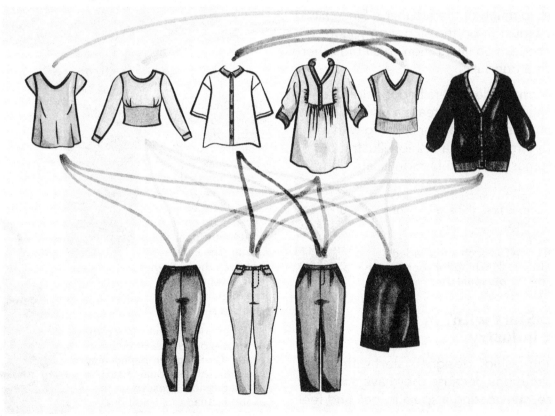

Rendered flat sketches make merchandising an easier task. The multiple lines in the image above represent how many variations can create different outfits within a small collection.

Scan this QR code to watch a free video of how the garment industry uses flat garment sketches for merchandising magic:

Scan this QR code to watch a free video about the technicality level of the flat sketches in *The Fashion Design Book:*

Which To Start with: a Fashion Illustration or a Flat Sketch?

You may start with either the fashion illustration or the flat sketch. The starting point may vary based on the usage or your preference.

This book is focused on flats, although you can also use the library of sketches for fashion illustrations.

Scan this QR code to watch a free video of how to draw a fashion illustration for a portfolio using this book:

Scan this QR code to watch a free video of how to master fashion illustration rendering:

Which To Start with? For a Portfolio & Personal Use

For a portfolio, you may start with the fashion illustration because it is the largest item on an artboard in the portfolio. For example, if you draw an evening gown that has a very full skirt, it may take up much of the artboard. Since all of the items must fit on the artboard, you may start with the fashion illustration so all the other parts can fit around it.

However, many designers find it helpful to start with flat sketches to create a visual closer to actual proportions. I prefer starting with a flat sketch before moving to a fashion illustration, and many times I skip the fashion illustration.

Scan this QR code to watch a free video about which comes first, flat sketches or fashion illustrations:

Scan this QR code to watch a free video about flat garment sketching for your fashion design portfolio or personal use:

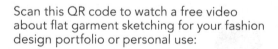

Which To Start with? In the Garment Industry

Many high-fashion designers start with fashion illustrations because they have an artistic appearance, showcasing a specific look and feel in the styling.

Many designers working for mainstream clothing brands only draw flat sketches and often skip fashion illustrations. Creating fashion illustrations is an extra step that many brands

do not require. In some cases, a designer may create a minimal amount of fashion illustrations for presentation purposes.

As software for fashion design continually improves, more companies are using 3D software that presents the garments on models. This gives a full-body image similar to that of a fashion illustration but more realistic. The 3D software can also create flat sketches which appear more 3-dimensional. In companies that are using 3D software, these more realistic images replace standard flat sketches and fashion illustrations.

Scan this QR code to watch a free video about the debate of fashion illustration versus flat garment sketches in the industry:

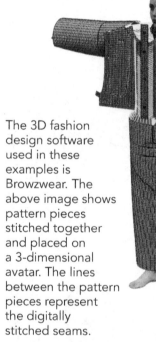

The 3D fashion design software used in these examples is Browzwear. The above image shows pattern pieces stitched together and placed on a 3-dimensional avatar. The lines between the pattern pieces represent the digitally stitched seams.

To the right is the same outfit as above, but dressed on the avatar. Clothing companies may use the 3-dimensional image of the garment dressed on the avatar instead of a traditional flat garment sketch. 3D design software such as Browzwear offers an excellent visual appearance of the garment. The more realistic image helps all departments within the company visualize the garments before they are created.

3D Images are courtesy of Browzwear.
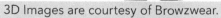

Fabric

Artboards within a portfolio should include fabric swatches of the main materials of the garment's exterior. The size should be a minimum of 2" x 2" (5 cm x 5 cm) unless another requirement is listed. If your portfolio is digital, scan photos of the fabrics to showcase them.

During the fabric selection process, a key characteristic to review is the drape of the fabric. The drape refers to how the fabric hangs. A fabric with less drape has more fullness and stands away from the body. A fabric with a high drape is slinky and hangs closer to the body.

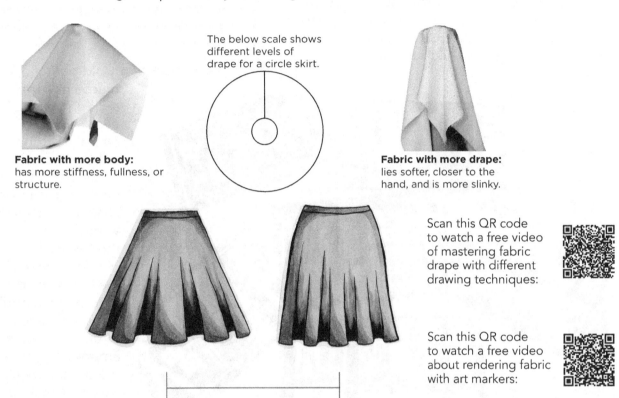

The below scale shows different levels of drape for a circle skirt.

Fabric with more body: has more stiffness, fullness, or structure.

Fabric with more drape: lies softer, closer to the hand, and is more slinky.

Scan this QR code to watch a free video of mastering fabric drape with different drawing techniques:

Scan this QR code to watch a free video about rendering fabric with art markers:

High/Full Body

High/Soft Drape

The amount of drape in the fabric will significantly affect the silhouette and the appearance of the style. Before selecting your fabrics, imagine how the style you have designed will look in that fabric.

Creating Artboards & Portfolios

After all four items have been created or determined (inspiration, fashion illustration, flat sketch, and fabric swatches), cut them out and create an artboard in your portfolio. In addition to having all four items on your artboard, to create a cohesive collection each style within your portfolio should have the same look and feel. Sometimes, you may have multiple collections with multiple looks. Examples could be a "vacation collection" or a "business casual collection."

Creating a portfolio or artboards in your design process is an excellent way to envision your designs before bringing them to life, even if it is not for a fashion school application or professional job portfolio. Use this process to create a collection of clothes for yourself or your clients that mix and match well to offer a cohesive appearance.

Scan this QR code to watch a free video of how to assemble an artboard for a portfolio:

About My Portfolio

Here is a glimpse into my past. For my fashion school application portfolio, I did my best drawing fashion illustrations and flat sketches. I included fabric swatches and inspiration. I sewed around 50 garments throughout my high school years and included most of these photos in my portfolio to showcase my sewing talents. My Dad took photos of me while I was modeling all the items I sewed. However, I knew they did not create a "cohesive" collection.

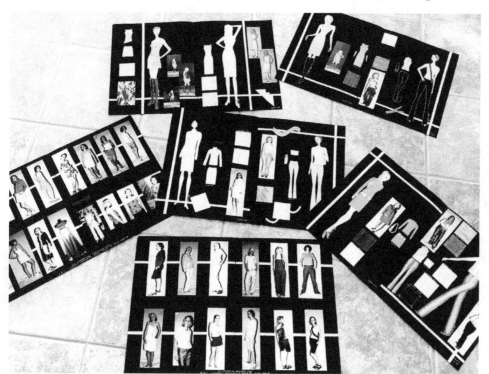

Above are some artboards from my fashion design portfolio from 1999. This was a school admittance design portfolio. In addition to standard artboards, I included many photos of items I designed and sewed during my high school years.

I had no idea how my portfolio compared with other people's portfolios. I waited months to find out if I was accepted to the fashion design program. It felt like ages as I waited, and I eagerly checked the mailbox every day after school.

One day, I went out to the mailbox and saw a letter from the Fashion Institute of Technology (FIT). I remember this day like it was yesterday. I ripped open the letter. It was an acceptance letter! My dream was coming true! I could not believe it! I started crying tears of joy. I had worked so hard for it, and it was actually happening.

I want you to have that moment of happiness, too, whether it means getting accepted to fashion school or having your designs turn out precisely as you envisioned.

The journey of creating can be enhanced by moving the ideas out of your head onto paper. Drawing your designs is the first step in the visualization process to turn those ideas into reality.

Looking back at my old portfolio, I see how much I have grown in my skills and experience. I even missed one of the four critical items needed on an artboard, which I discuss in this book. Can you see what critical item I did not include on my artboards? Watch the video through the QR link below to find out. The illustrations were the best I could do at the time. Now, my skills are much stronger, as displayed throughout this book. It's empowering to see my progress. It reminds me that we all have the potential to improve. We can all learn new skills and strengthen our weaknesses. I am still learning!

And if you are talented in drawing, try developing new skills to see what other areas might interest you. Even drawing flat garment sketches enables you to master technical knowledge different from fashion illustration.

As you practice more and more, sketching will become easier, and you will improve. Additionally, your design sense will improve with consistent practice.

Embrace the journey of learning and growing. Take steps toward achieving your dreams.

To see more of my school portfolio and compare the differences to my professional portfolio, scan this QR code to watch a free video with an example:

How To Use *The Fashion Design Book*

This book will teach you how to sketch and design clothes. It will guide you through the process with free step-by-step videos (through QR codes).

Except for the few extra blank pages to add to your library, this is not a sketchbook where you draw your designs inside the book.

There are two methods of using this book:

1) As a template for tracing;

2) As a reference to see how to draw the designs.

If you are a beginner, the tracing method is beneficial until you understand sketching proportions. Use this book in conjunction with tracing paper or thin marker paper for this method. The tracing or thin marker paper is see-through. Place the tracing or marker paper on the style details and silhouettes to draw your designs.

Then, cut out the styles you have designed. Add them to your artboard or sketchbook.

If you plan to render the images with art markers, use thin marker paper. I recommend a weight of 70 g/m² (18 lb.). Tracing paper will suffice if you keep it black and white.

You may also use a photocopier to copy your own black-and-white sketches onto regular or marker paper to render them with different colors, enhancing the design selection process. A photocopier may also resize your sketches for a portfolio to make the flat sketches fit on the artboard or in a sketchbook.

As you become more advanced, you will likely move to the second method of simply referencing the sketches as needed and draw without tracing.

The entire book is a mix-and-match library of sketches to assist you in creating your designs. This book is a "designer's toolbox" with everything you need to select the parts you want. For example, choose one neckline, sleeve design, and dress silhouette to create a unique style.

Besides all of the sketches in this book, another valuable part of the book is the terminology of the design details or silhouettes. Studying these names and terms used throughout this book will significantly increase your knowledge in designing garments.

When a dash separates a name, it means that the preceding words could be used at the beginning of the name. For example, "Dolman - Low" could also be called "Low Dolman." This concept with the dash is used throughout the book, so similar styles are next to each other in alphabetical order.

When there is more than one name, secondary names are in parenthesis. For example, "Dolman - Low (Batwing)" could also be referred to as its secondary name, "Batwing."

Although I tried to include the most common silhouettes and design details, fashion is ever-changing. That is why at the end of the chapters, there are empty pages for you to add your favorite silhouettes and design details.

You will notice that some chapters have specific design details, making the styles more than just a lined silhouette. Please use these style details as a guide, and do not take them literally. These style details show you how to draw them. For example, for a design detail like gathering or shirring, view styles with the gathering to understand how to draw gathering. Gathering or shirring is a method that takes a high volume of fabric to create puckers and fullness. Apply the gathering to the location you wish.

You can change any design of the garments in this book. You might like one aspect of one style and something else of another. Or you might use one part in a different location. Get creative with what is here. Mix and match as you like. Your designs will start to flow once you begin.

I highly recommend scanning the QR code below and signing up for your exclusive access to the Free Video Vault, so you can continually learn how to render and use this book most beneficially.

Scan this QR code to watch a free video with an example of how to use this book:

To sign up for the Free Video Vault, where there are many videos that are not shown through QR codes in this book, go here:

Let the Designing Begin!

Croquis

The croquis in this book is 7 ½ heads tall. Most people are between 7 and 8 heads tall. The standard figure is an excellent starting point for portfolios or garment industry use.

What is a standard body type? The industry-standard body type is based on averages across a range of people, varying from company to company. Companies use the standard size in fittings to evaluate clothes.

Every person has different body measurements, and I encourage you to draw your customized croquis. Just know that the "standard body type" does not mean it is the perfect body. YOU are **perfect** exactly as you are!

When you watch the videos through the QR codes below, you will find additional croquis to download, including standard, midsize and curvy/plus size options.

Creating customized croquis will better represent your shapes. To do this, place a piece of paper over the standard croquis and expand or reduce any parts you think more accurately represent you. Watch the videos through the QR codes below for a full tutorial.

You may also take photos of yourself and print them on letter (8 ½" x 11") or A4 paper size or view them on a tablet. Then, apply those proportions to the croquis. I show this in a step-by-step process in the free video through the QR code below.

Once you have customized your croquis and are pleased with it, draw it, cut it, and paste it on the following blank page that says, "My Customized Croquis."

Scan this QR code to watch a free video on how to customize a croquis to your shape:

Scan this QR code to watch a free video to learn how to use the book with your customized croquis:

Main Croquis

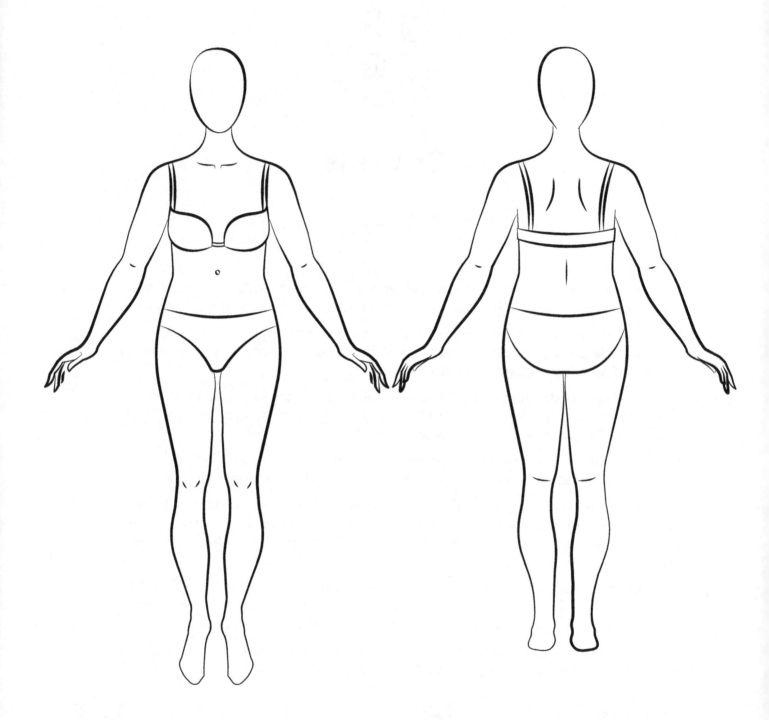

Note: the back view of the croquis is not typically used in drawing flat garment sketches. See the QR code videos on page 169 to learn how to draw the back view of garments without a croquis.

My Customized Croquis

Scan the QR code on page 21 to watch a free video on how to customize a croquis to your shape.

My Customized Croquis

Necklines, Collars, and Hoods

The designing begins! This is the fun part of mixing and matching all the options in this book. Choose your desired neckline, collar, sleeve, cuff, and top silhouette to create tops. Mix and match these with skirts, and you will create dresses.

Scan this QR code now to learn how to mix and match the different parts of the garment to create your unique designs:

Additionally, there are collars for blazers, jackets, and coats. Finally, there are hoods at the end of the chapter. Mix and match these with other silhouettes and design details found throughout the book. At the end of each section, you will notice an area to draw your favorite silhouettes or designs to customize your library. You may draw directly in the book or cut and paste sketches into your customized pages.

To design, you may start with any section in this book. The book is laid out according to the top part of garments and then continues toward the bottom of an outfit. If you are unsure where to start, pick any silhouette that inspires you.

Necklines

Asymmetric

Ballerina

Boat
(Bateau)

Bottle

Bottle - High with Darts

Camisole with
Spaghetti Straps

Cowl

Crew
with Ribbing

Diamond

Drawstring

Florentine

Funnel

Gathered

Grecian

Halter - Tall

Necklines

Halter Strap

Halter
The neck shape can vary.

Henley

Horseshoe

Keyhole
The cut-out shape can vary.

Notched

Off-the-Shoulder

One-shoulder

Oval

Petal

Plunge

Plunge Sweetheart

Queen Anne

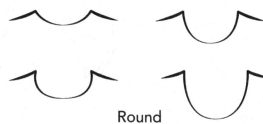

Round

Necklines

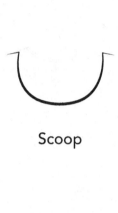

Scoop

Slashed

Slit

Square

Square with
Criss-cross Straps

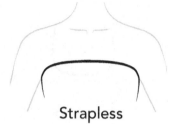

Strapless

Surplice
(Wrap)

Sweetheart

Trapeze

Tucked

Turtleneck - Fitted

Turtleneck - Oversized

U-neck

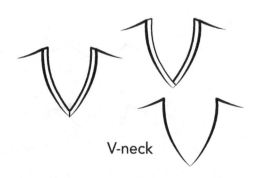

V-neck

Yoke Boat

Collars for Shirts

Asymmetric

Banded Stand

Bow

Chelsea

Closed   Open

Standard Collar with Half-moon Stand

Eton

Horseshoe

Imperial

Jabot

Johnny

Loop

Mandarin

Mitered

Narrow Spread

Collars for Shirts

Notched

Peter Pan

Peter Pan - Cornered

Pinned

Poet

Pointed
(Barrymore)

Polo

Puritan

Round

Sailor
(Middy)

Short Button-down

Stand-away

Closed

Open

Standard Collar with Stand

Wide Spread
(Cutaway)

Wing
(Tuxedo)

My Customized Necklines and Collars for Shirts

Collars for Blazers

Curved Collar - Plunging

Napoleon

Notched Lapel - Chesterfield

Notched Lapel - Clover

Notched Lapel - Half Clover

Notched Lapel - Plunging

Open

Closed

Notched Lapel - Standard

Peak Lapel - Fish Mouth

Peak Lapel - Framed

Peak Lapel - L-shaped

Peak Lapel - Plunging Double-breasted

Peak Lapel - Rounded

Collars for Blazers

Peak Lapel
(Pointed Lapel)

Peak Lapel and
Rounded Collar

Semi-peak

Shawl

Shawl - Notched

T-shaped

Tab Collar

Ulster

My Customized Collars for Blazers

Collars for Jackets and Coats

Flared Spread

Notched Lapel - Oversized

Notched Lapel and
Double-breasted

Notched Lapel with a
Wide-spread Collar

Notched Lapel with a
Rounded Collar

Notched Lapel

Peak Lapel and
Double-breasted

Shawl - Square

Shawl - Oversized
and Angled

Standing Collar

Closed

Open

Turtle Neck - Oversized Collar

Collars for Jackets and Coats

Winged Lapel   Wrap with Internal Facing
(No Collar)

My Customized Collars for Jackets and Coats

Hoods

Brim Along the Face Opening

Faux Fur Parka

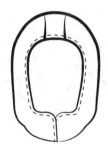

High Center Front

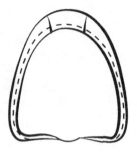

Oversized

Pullover - Fitted

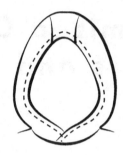

Pullover - Oversized

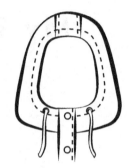

Utility Style

My Customized Hoods

Sleeves and Cuffs

Sleeve shapes are ever-changing in fashion. The silhouettes and style details on sleeves can mark an era, for example, the huge puff sleeves of the 80s prom dresses. There are so many sleeve designs. If you do not see your exact design in the book, look for the closest design or silhouette and change it to how you envision it. When designing, you can always change the styling to make it unique.

Consider the fabric you choose and how the drape of the fabric (the way it hangs) should be drawn. This can greatly affect the sleeve shape and dimension. If the fabric has more fullness in the drape, it will stand away from the body. If the fabric is slinky, it will hang close to the body.

Cuffs are a beautiful way to add styling to blouses, dresses, blazers, jackets, and coats. Refer to the cuffs in this chapter for all of these items. If you design cuffs for jackets and coats, enlarge them slightly to represent the larger outer layer.

The enlarged images in the section of the cuffs highlight the details that the patternmaker, technical designer, product developer, and factory will reference. The enlarged image is an example of a detail that a designer would show in a tech pack for the technical execution of the garment. Generally, this cuff and placket detail is on the back of the garment.

Watch this free video to learn more about drawing styles with sleeves and detailed images of the cuffs:

Length Options for Sleeves

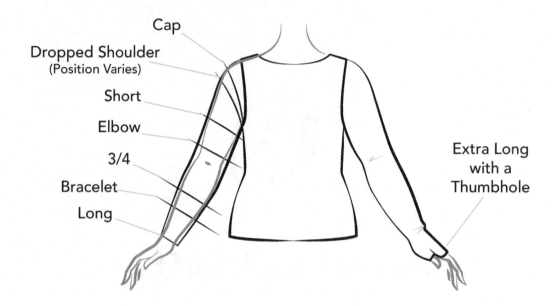

Cap

Dropped Shoulder
(Position Varies)

Short

Elbow

3/4

Bracelet

Long

Extra Long
with a
Thumbhole

Basic Sleeve Lengths

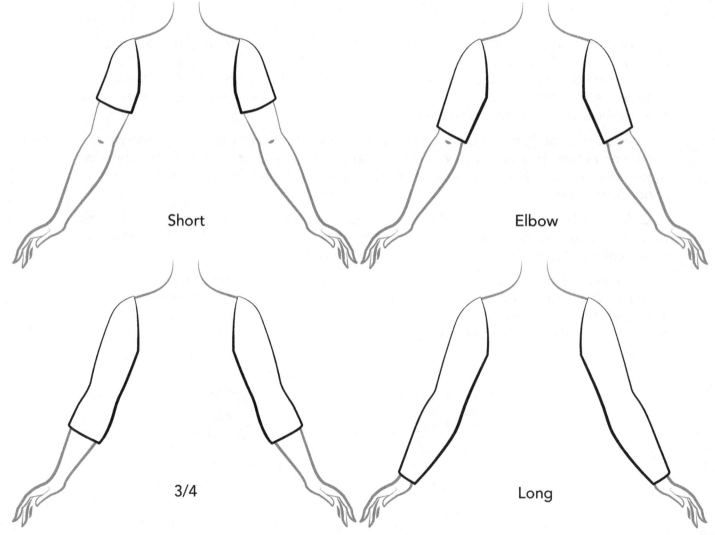

Short

Elbow

3/4

Long

Sleeves

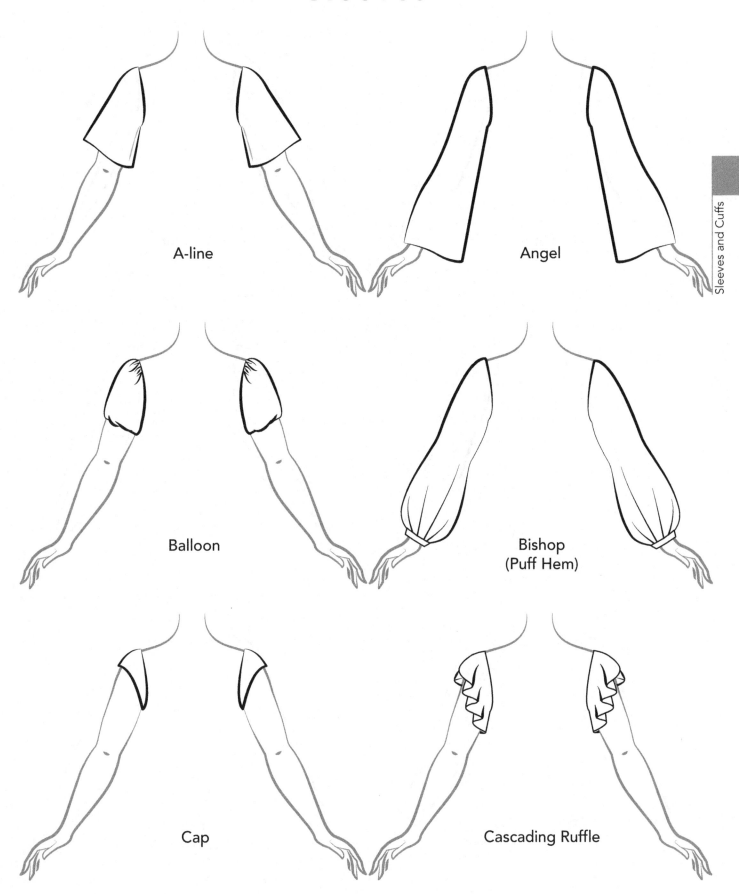

A-line

Angel

Balloon

Bishop
(Puff Hem)

Cap

Cascading Ruffle

Sleeves

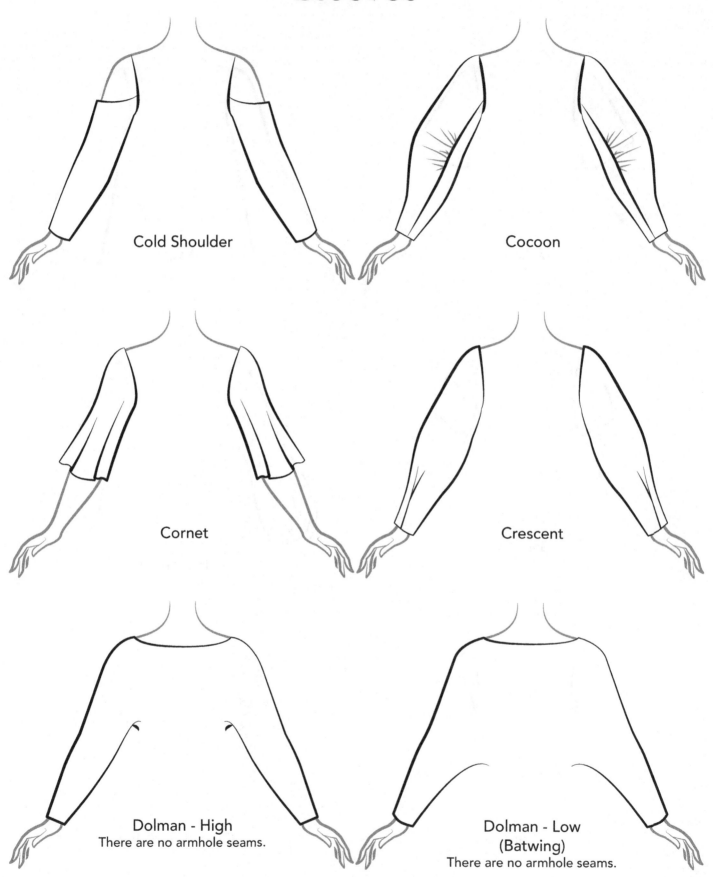

Cold Shoulder

Cocoon

Cornet

Crescent

Dolman - High
There are no armhole seams.

Dolman - Low
(Batwing)
There are no armhole seams.

Sleeves

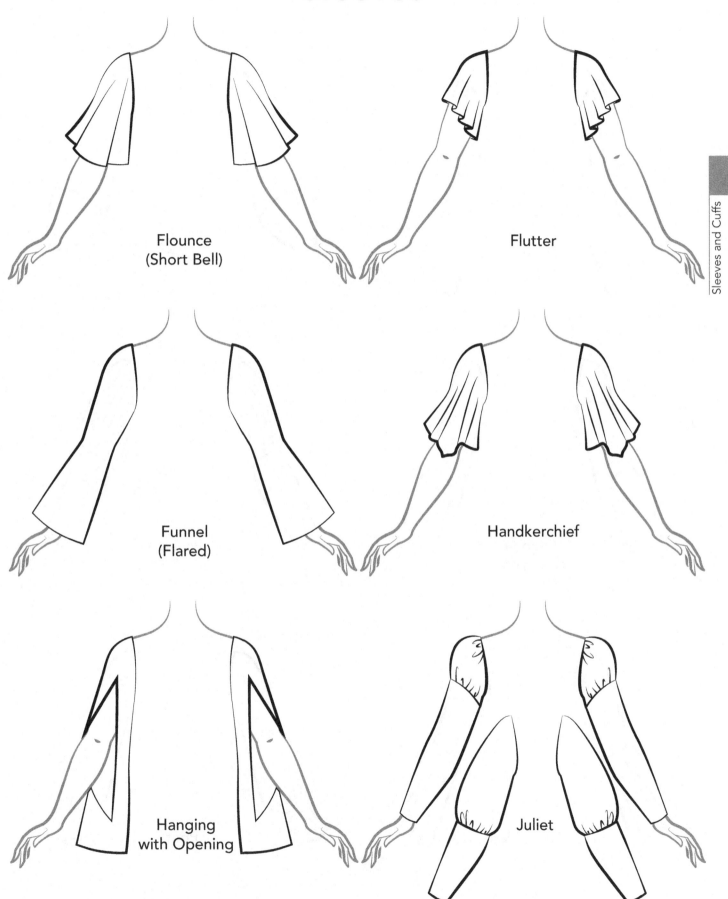

Flounce
(Short Bell)

Flutter

Funnel
(Flared)

Handkerchief

Hanging
with Opening

Juliet

Sleeves

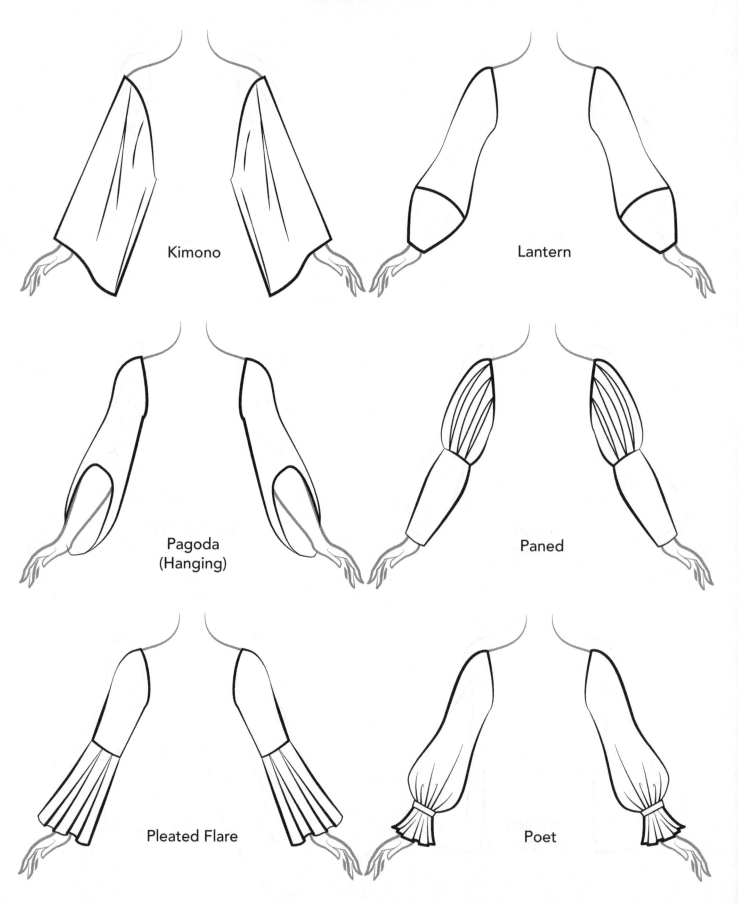

Kimono

Lantern

Pagoda
(Hanging)

Paned

Pleated Flare

Poet

Sleeves

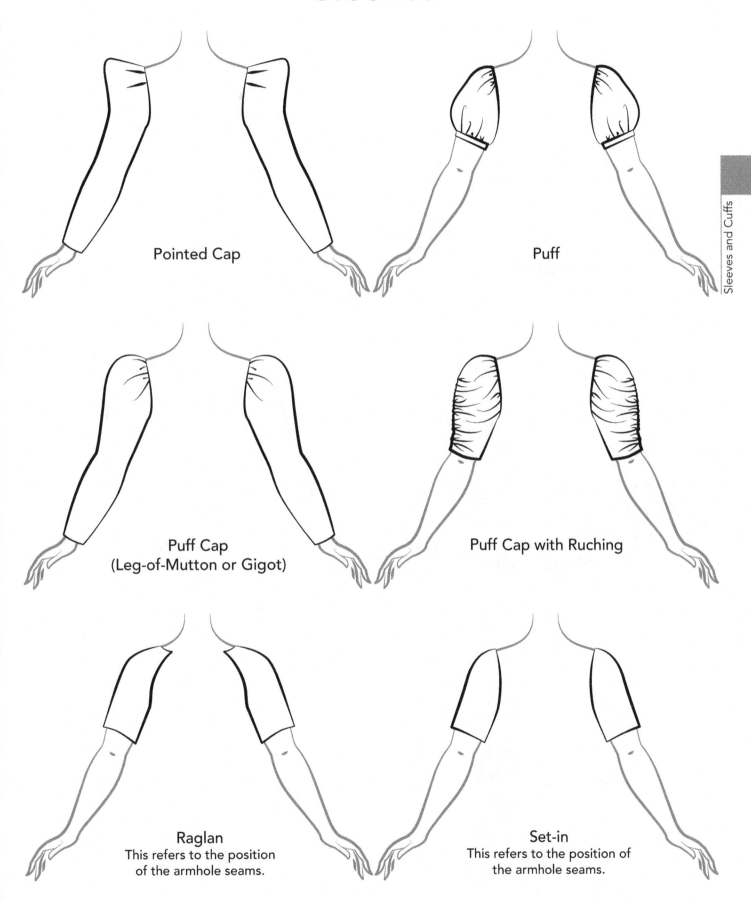

Pointed Cap

Puff

Puff Cap
(Leg-of-Mutton or Gigot)

Puff Cap with Ruching

Raglan
This refers to the position
of the armhole seams.

Set-in
This refers to the position
of the armhole seams.

Sleeves

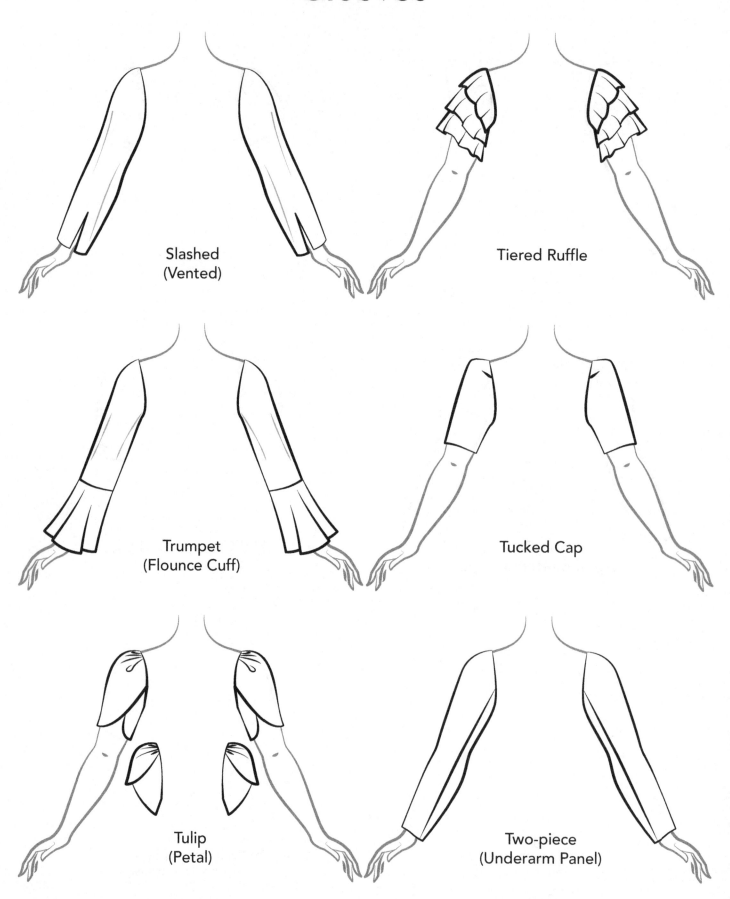

Slashed
(Vented)

Tiered Ruffle

Trumpet
(Flounce Cuff)

Tucked Cap

Tulip
(Petal)

Two-piece
(Underarm Panel)

Sleeves

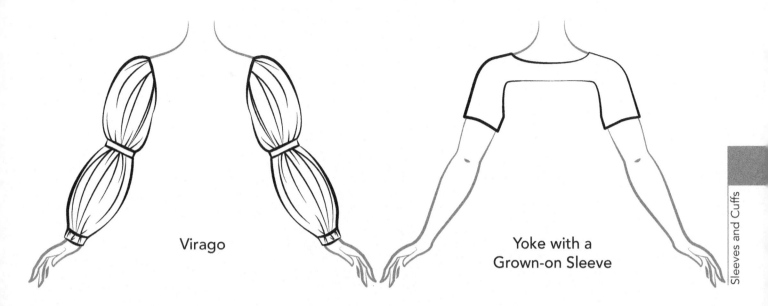

Virago

Yoke with a
Grown-on Sleeve

My Customized Sleeves

My Customized Sleeves

Sleeve Cuffs and Plackets

Cuffs with plackets are the back view of the garment.

Close Up

To Scale

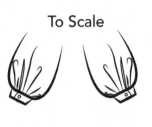 

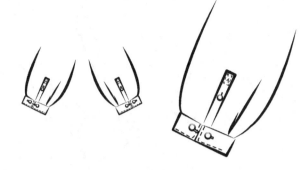

Banded Cuff with Snap and a Bishop Sleeve with Faced Keyhole Placket

Convertible Cuff with Placket and Pleats
This can be worn with cuff links
or as a standard shirt cuff.

Elastic Cuff with a Bishop Sleeve

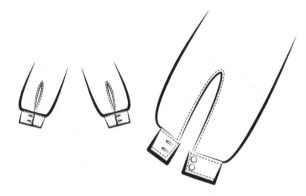

Faced Keyhole Placket with Cuff

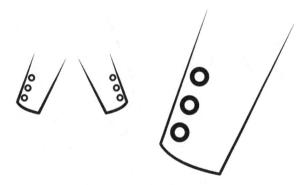

Faux Closure

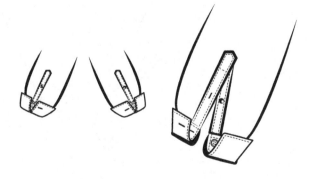

Folded Cuff with Placket

Sleeve Cuffs and Plackets

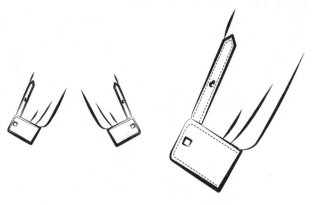

French Cuff (Cuff Link)
with Placket and Pleats

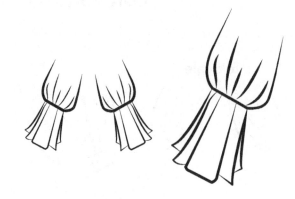

Frilled Cuff

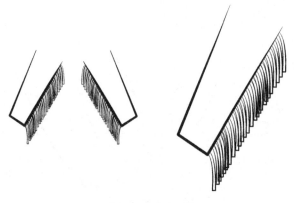

Fringed Cuff

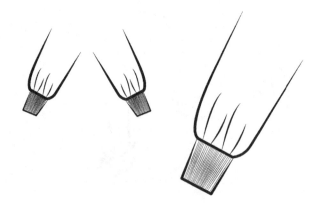

Knit Cuff

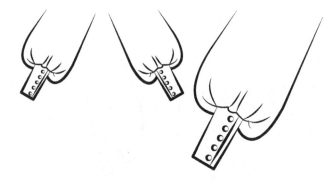

Long Buttoned or Snapped Cuff
with Bishop Sleeve

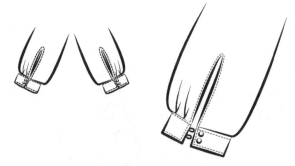

Loop Closure Cuff with Faced
Keyhole Placket and Pleats

Sleeve Cuffs and Plackets

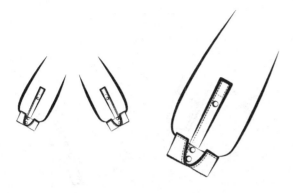

Portofino Cuff

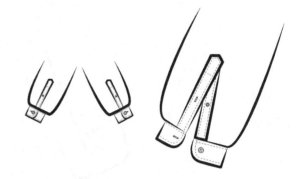

Rounded Cuff with Placket

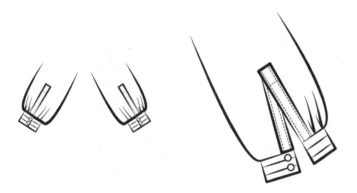

Seamed Cuff with Placket and Pleats

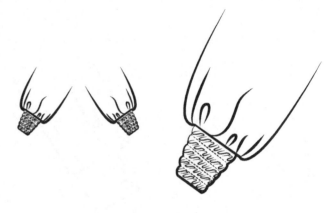

Smocked Cuff

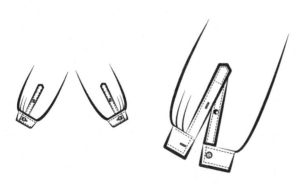

Standard Shirt Cuff (Barrel Cuff)
with Placket and Pleats

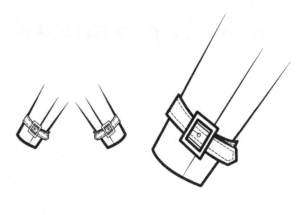

Strap with a Buckle

Sleeve Cuffs and Plackets

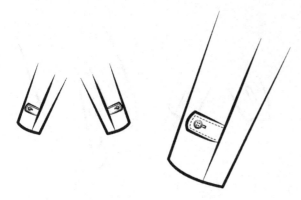

Tab with a Button

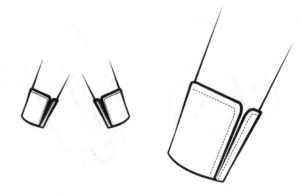

Turn-up Cuff

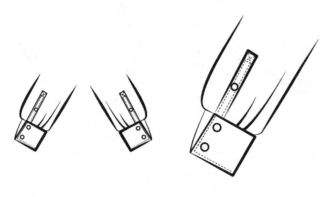

2-Button or Snap Cuff with Placket
and Pleats

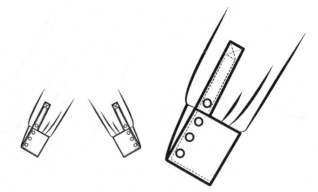

3-Button or Snap Cuff with Placket
and Pleats

My Customized Cuffs and Plackets

Darts, Pintucks, Pleats, Gathering, and Ruffles

Style details including darts, pintucks, pleats, gathering, and ruffles help set styles apart and create unique design details. These design details can help achieve a better fit. They also create different silhouettes. Learn more about these topics and how to draw these design details in the free videos through the QR codes below.

Watch this video to learn the importance of darts and princess seams in fashion design and how to draw them:

Watch this video to understand the difference between gathering, shirring, and ruching. I'll also show you how to draw them:

Watch this video to practice drawing pleats to create fullness:

Watch this video to practice drawing ruffles and full hemlines:

Common Locations for Darts, Pleats, and Princess Seams on Bodices

Armhole Darts

Armscye
Princess Seams

Center Front
Angled Darts

Center Front
Horizontal Darts

Double
Princess Seams

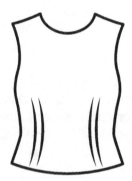

Double
Waist Darts

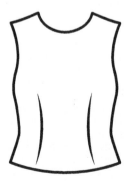

Fisheye
Waist Darts

French Darts

Neckline Darts
or Pleats

Common Locations for Darts, Pleats, and Princess Seams on Bodices

Neckline
Princess Seams

Side Bust Darts

Shoulder Darts
or Pleats

Shoulder
Princess Seams

Vertical Shoulder
and Waist Darts

Vertical
Waist Darts

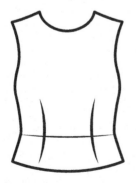

Vertical Waist Darts
with Waistline Seam

V-darts or
V-pleats

Wrap Bodice
with Darts or Pleats

Common Locations for Pintucks on Bodices

For fitted silhouettes, combine these with the darts and princess seam options.

Asymmetrical
Tucks

Horizontal
Tucks

Shoulder
Tucks

Vertical Center
Tucks

V-shaped
Pintucks

My Customized Darts and Pintucks

Types of Pleats

Accordion Pleats

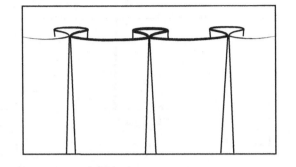

Box Pleats - Inverted

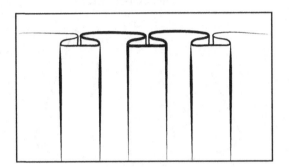

Box Pleats

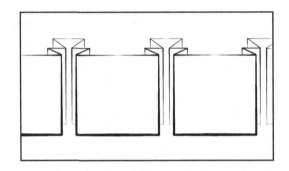

Box Pleats - Inverted Double

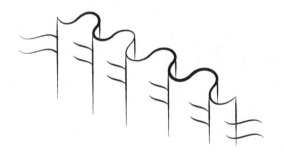

Cartridge Pleats

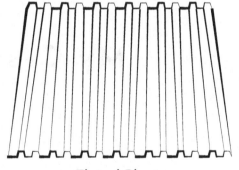

Fluted Pleats

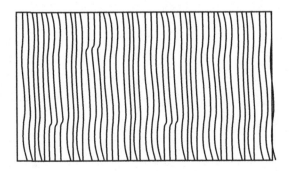

Fortuny Pleats

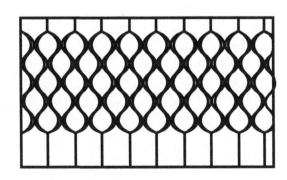

Honeycomb Pleats

Types of Pleats

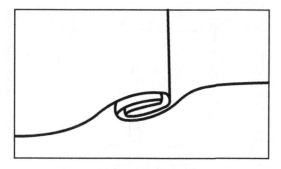

Rolled Pleats

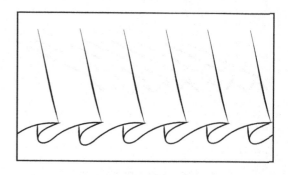

Side Pleats - Knife
(Hard-pressed)

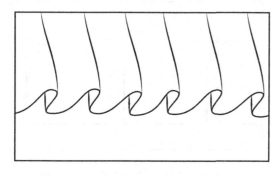

Side Pleats - Soft
(Unpressed)

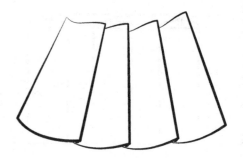

Side Pleats - Sunburst
(Directional)

My Customized Pleats

Drawing Pleats

Box Pleats

Step 1:

Step 2: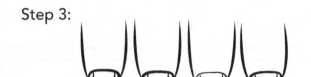

Step 3:

Final Aesthetic:

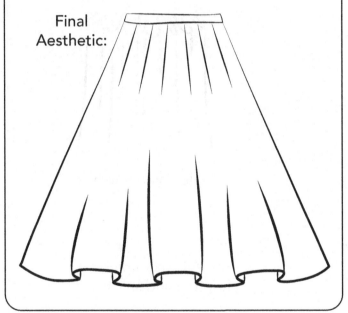

Side Pleats - Soft (Unpressed)

Step 1:

Step 2:

Step 3:

Side Pleats - Knife (Hard-pressed)

Step 1:

Step 2:

Step 3:

Tucks and Gathering

Tucks and Pintucks

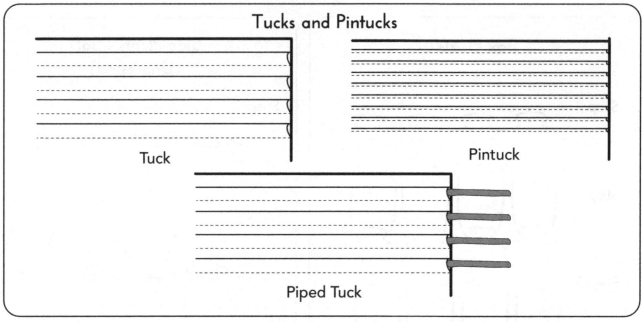

Tuck

Pintuck

Piped Tuck

Types of Gathering (Shirring or Ruching)

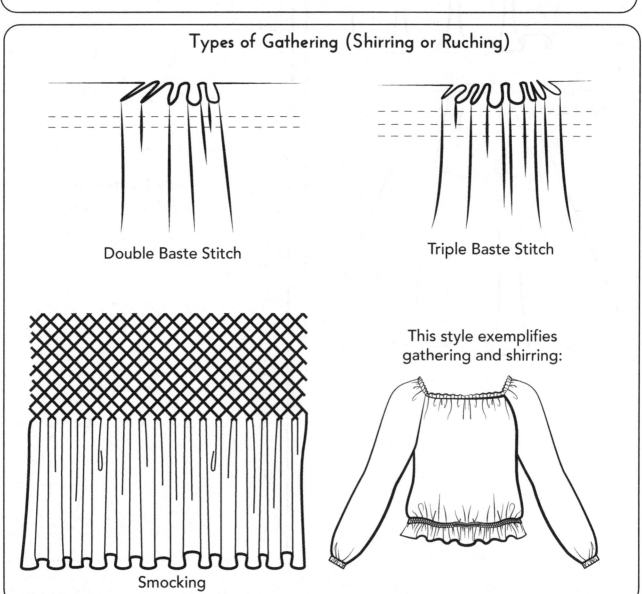

Double Baste Stitch

Triple Baste Stitch

Smocking

This style exemplifies gathering and shirring:

How To Draw Ruffles

Cascading Ruffle down the Center

Step 1:

Step 2: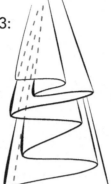

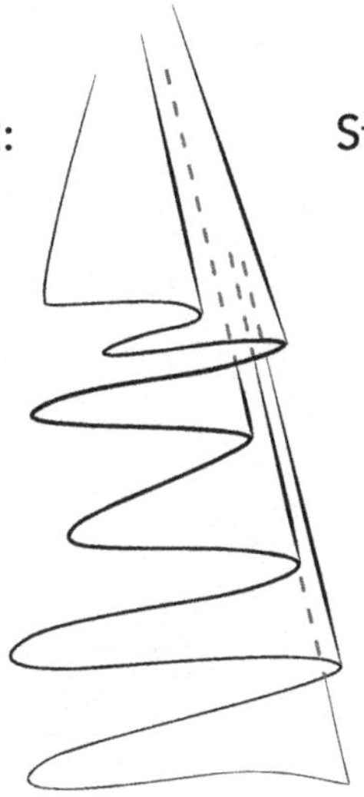

Step 3:

Step 4:

Cascading Ruffle from One Side

Step 1:

Step 2:

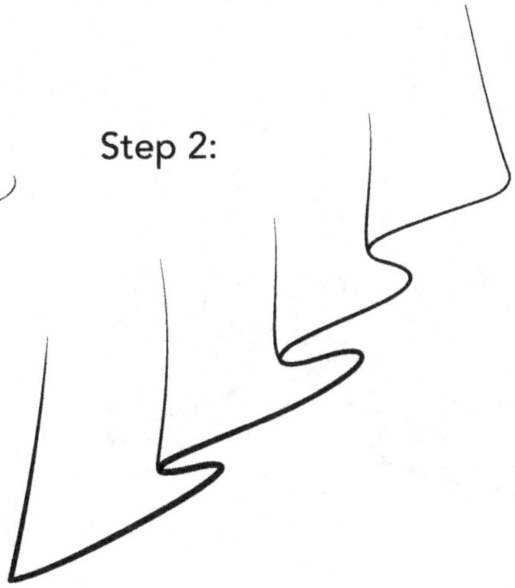

Step 3:

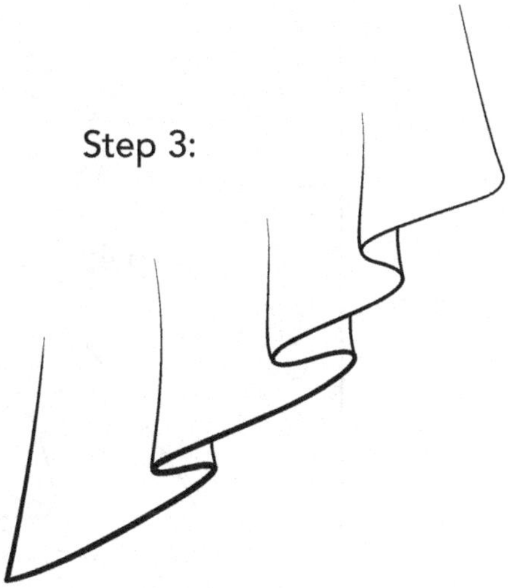

An Exampled of an A-symmetric Neckline with a Circular Cascading Ruffle:

An Exampled of an A-symmetric Neckline Ruffle with Gathering:

How To Draw Ruffles

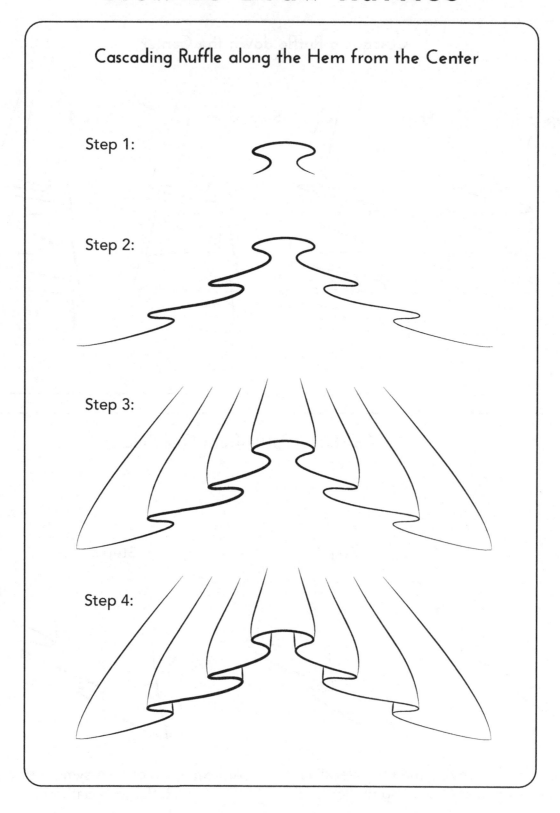

Cascading Ruffle along the Hem from the Center

Step 1:

Step 2:

Step 3:

Step 4:

How To Draw Ruffles

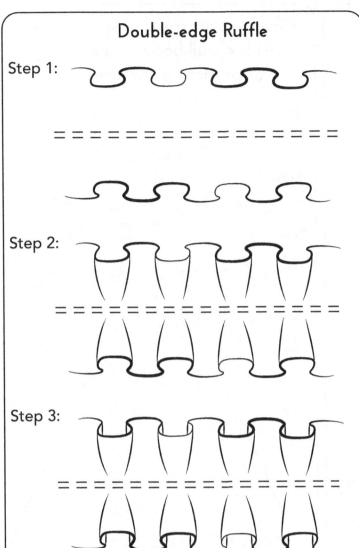

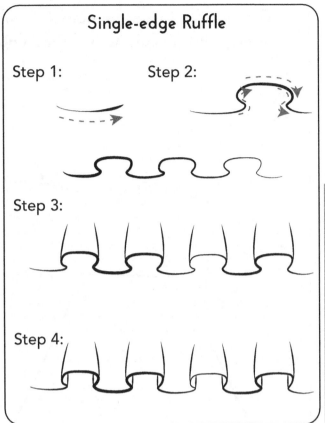

Double-edge Ruffle

Step 1:

Step 2:

Step 3:

Single-edge Ruffle

Step 1:

Step 2:

Step 3:

Step 4:

Practice Drawing Ruffles

Darts, Pintucks, Pleats, Gathering, and Ruffles

How To Draw Voluminous Hemlines

Circular Skirt from an above Hemline View with a High-body Drape Fabric

Step 1:

Step 2:

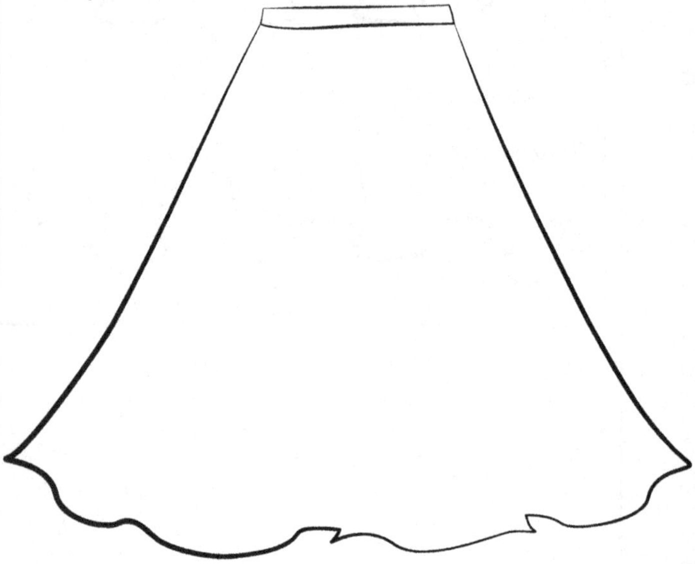

Step 3:

Circular Skirt from a Hemline View with a Full-body Drape Fabric (Symmetrical Appearance)

Step 1:

Step 2:

Step 3:

Step 4:

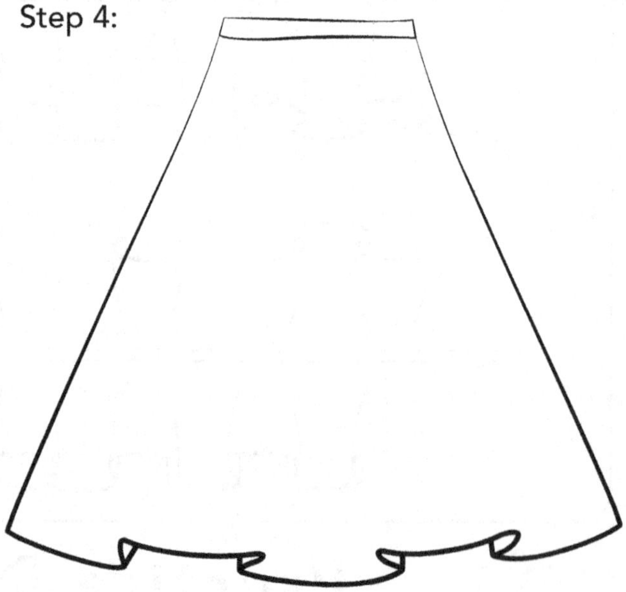

Step 5:

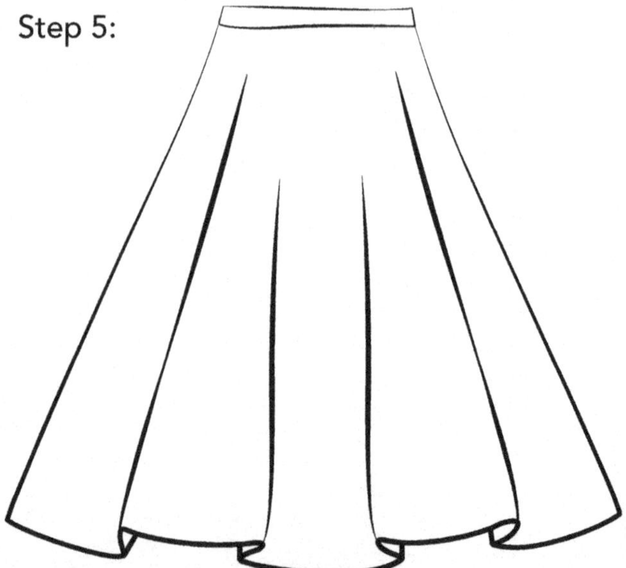

Tops

This chapter includes tops, mid-layers, and outer layers. This was the most challenging chapter to create because a wide variety of styles could be showcased. The designs include various details that could be used within a style.

You might look at these chapters and think, "These styles are already designed." Please do not take these styles literally. Use these styles to learn how to draw the design details like gathering, darts, ruffles, and draped fabrics. Get inspiration from the style details and apply these concepts to your styles.

If the style details overwhelm you, start by looking at the silhouette, which is the outside line of the style, to see if that is the direction you want to go. It might be a challenge at first, but you are a creative person. Once you start designing, there will be no stopping you.

After using these styles for the silhouette lines, select different necklines, collars, sleeves, and garment lengths. Draw your own design lines to create your unique styles.

What are design lines? A design line is a seam in the garment that is specific to a style. It makes the style unique. Design lines are often created to close darts on a sewing pattern. This process optimizes the fit of garments, and designers should consider this while designing. This concept of closing darts on a sewing pattern is called pattern manipulation, a patternmaking technique.

If you are not familiar with these patternmaking terms, scan this QR code to learn more about patternmaking terminology:

Then, scan this QR code to understand how design lines can optimize the fit of garments:

Every designer should watch this video!

Gain exclusive access to the Free Video Vault so you can continually learn more about design optimization for fit:

Length Options and Main Silhouettes for Tops

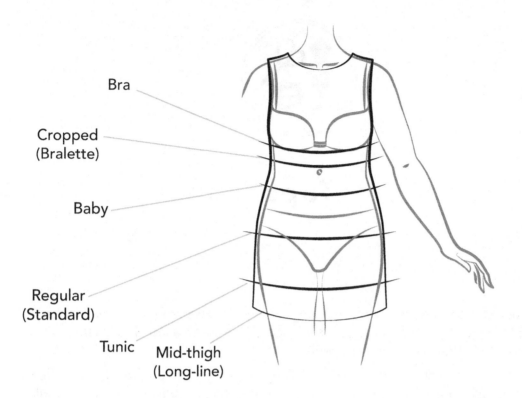

Bra

Cropped
(Bralette)

Baby

Regular
(Standard)

Tunic   Mid-thigh
(Long-line)

Main Silhouettes for Tops - Knits

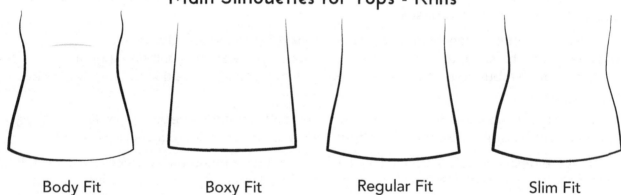

Body Fit   Boxy Fit   Regular Fit   Slim Fit

Main Silhouettes for Tops - Wovens
Dart locations can vary.
Darts may also be turned into princess seams, design lines, pleats, gathering, or tucks.

Boxy Fit   Regular Fit   Slim Fit

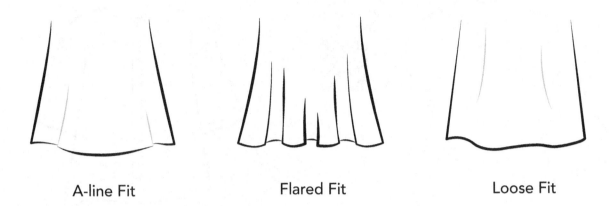

A-line Fit   Flared Fit   Loose Fit

My Customized Silhouettes for Tops

Tops

Styled Tops

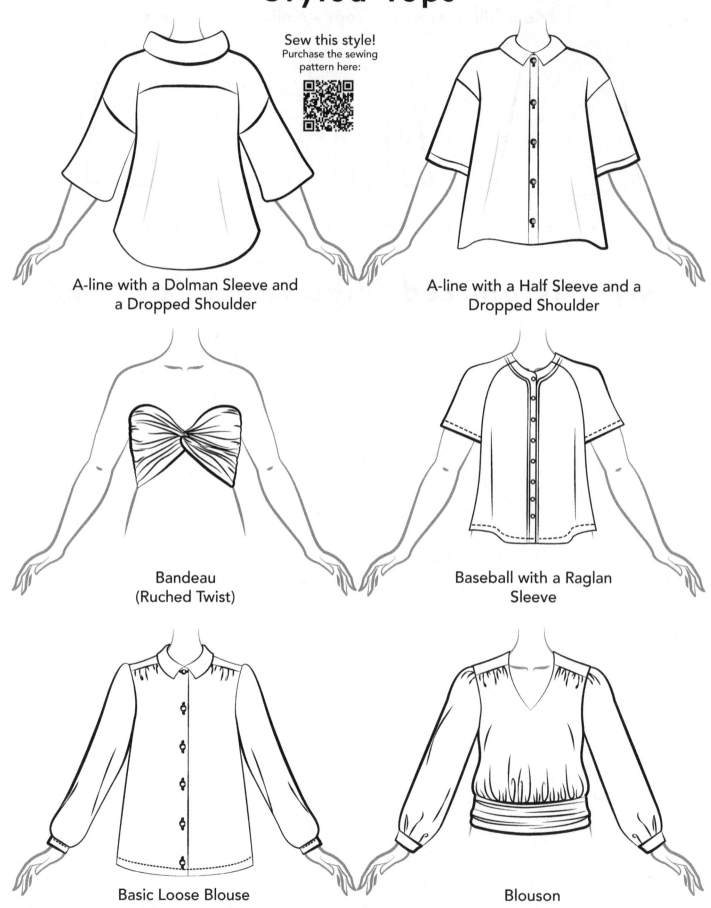

Sew this style!
Purchase the sewing pattern here:

A-line with a Dolman Sleeve and a Dropped Shoulder

A-line with a Half Sleeve and a Dropped Shoulder

Bandeau (Ruched Twist)

Baseball with a Raglan Sleeve

Basic Loose Blouse

Blouson

Styled Tops

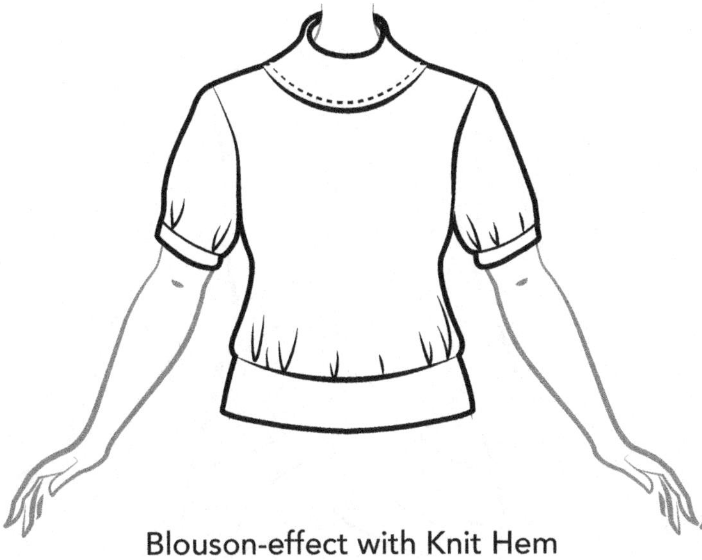

Blouson-effect with Knit Hem
Band and Cuffs

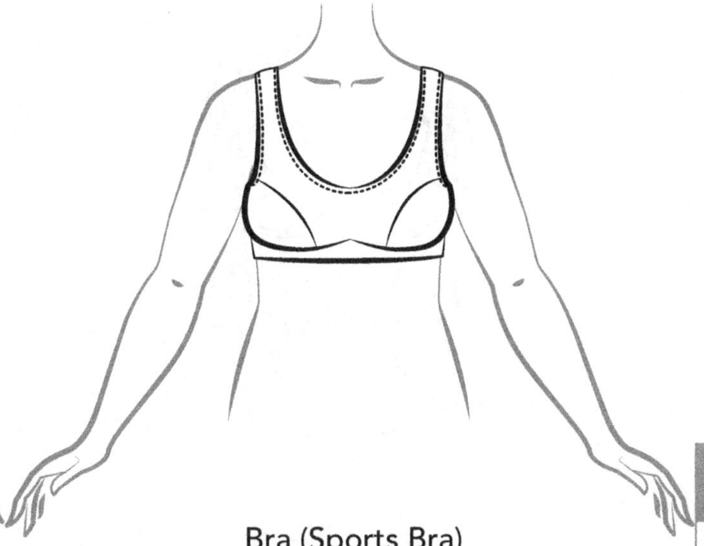

Bra (Sports Bra)

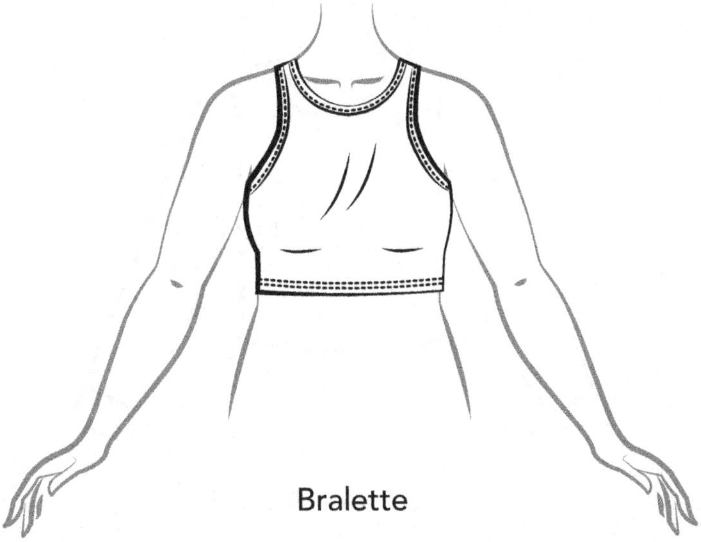

Bralette

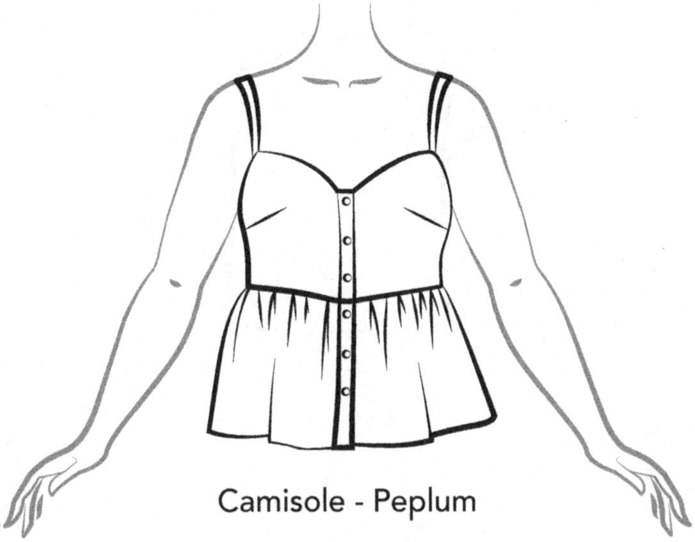

Camisole - Peplum

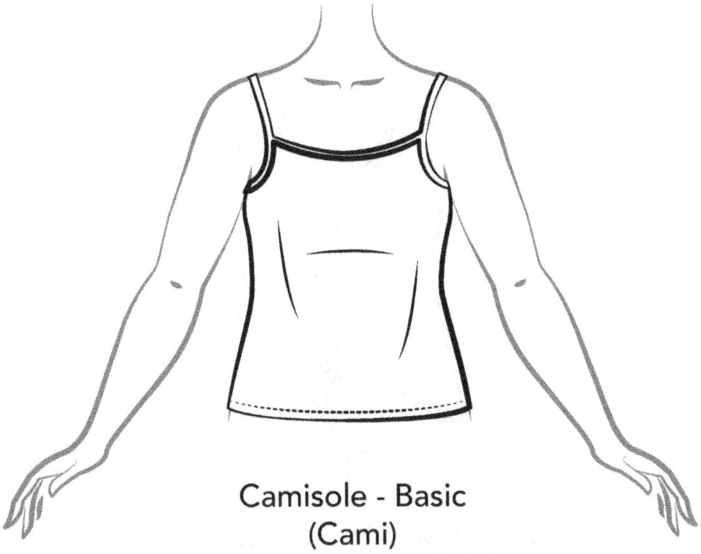

Camisole - Basic
(Cami)

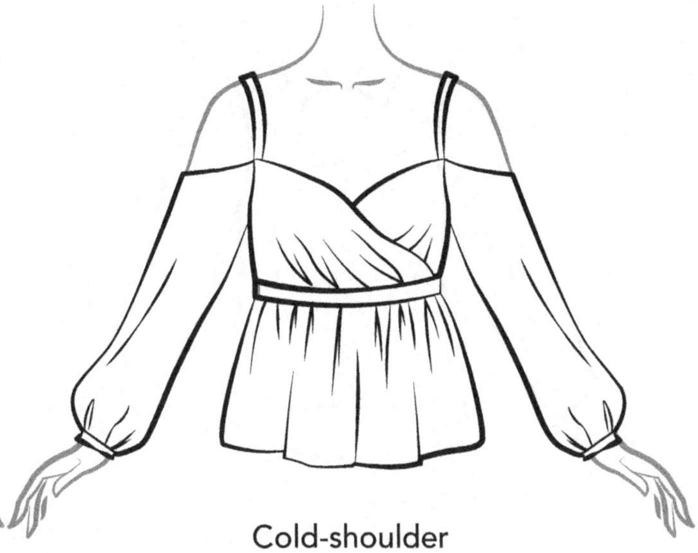

Cold-shoulder

Styled Tops

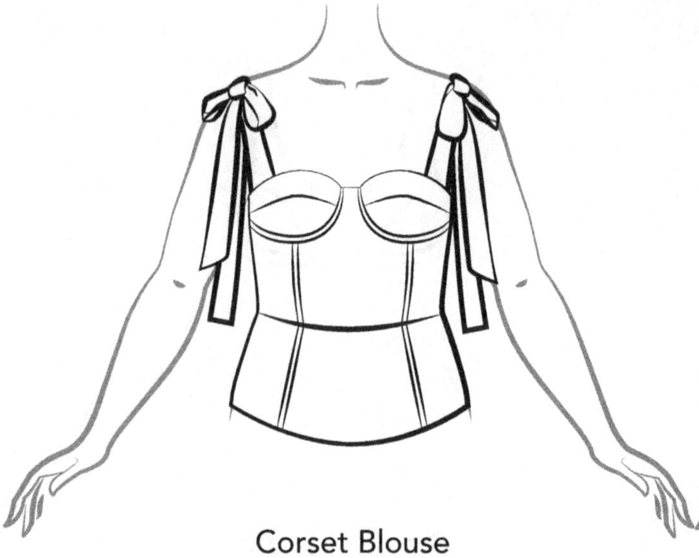

Corset Blouse

Criss-cross

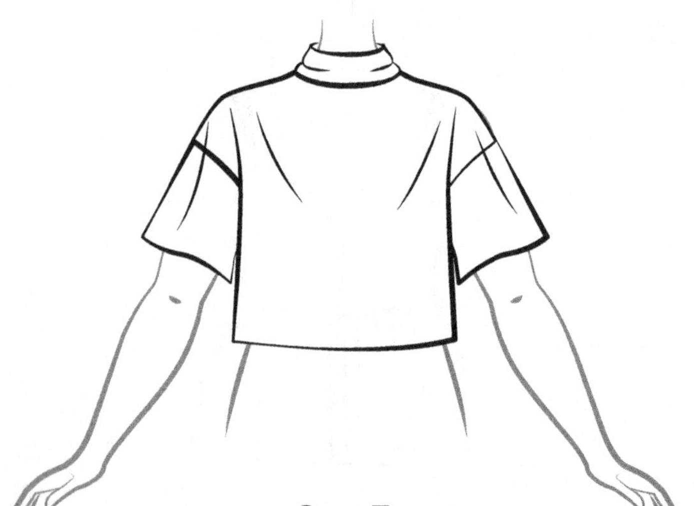

Crop Top

Crop Top - Midriff

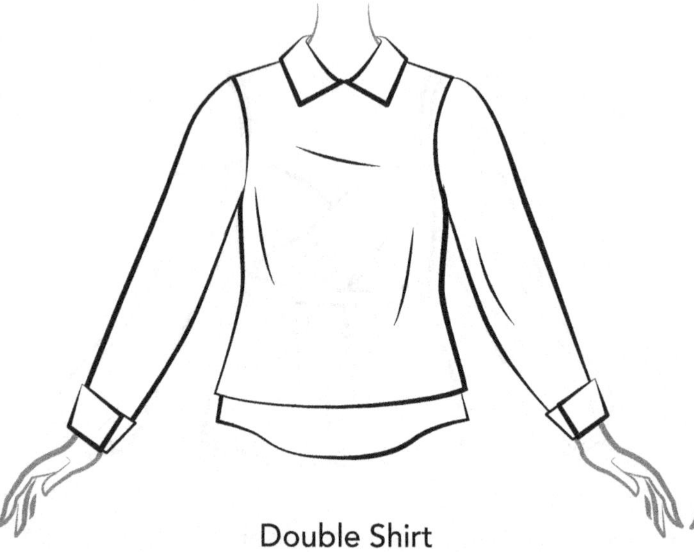

Double Shirt

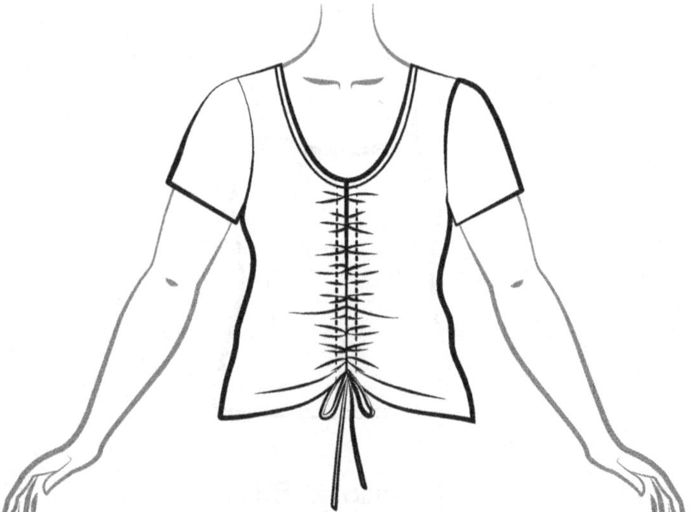

Drawstring - Vertical

Styled Tops

Drawstring Hemline with
a Dropped Shoulder

Empire Waistline with Gathering

Fitted Button-down

Gaucho

Gibson

Henley-inspired Button-down

Styled Tops

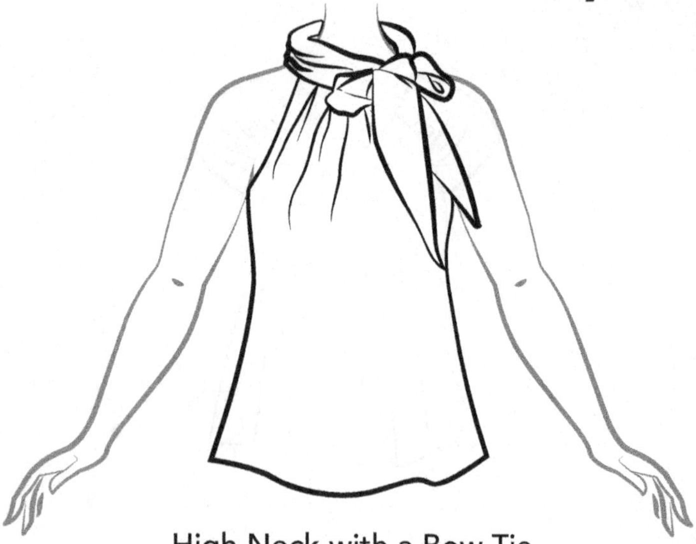

High Neck with a Bow Tie

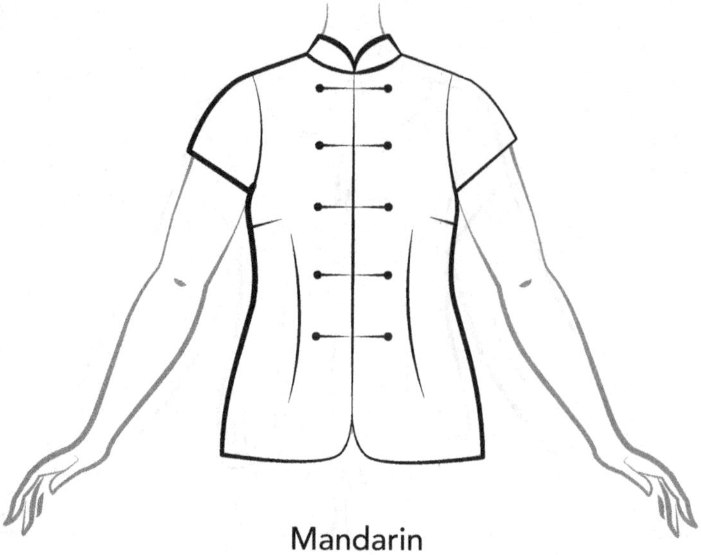

Mandarin

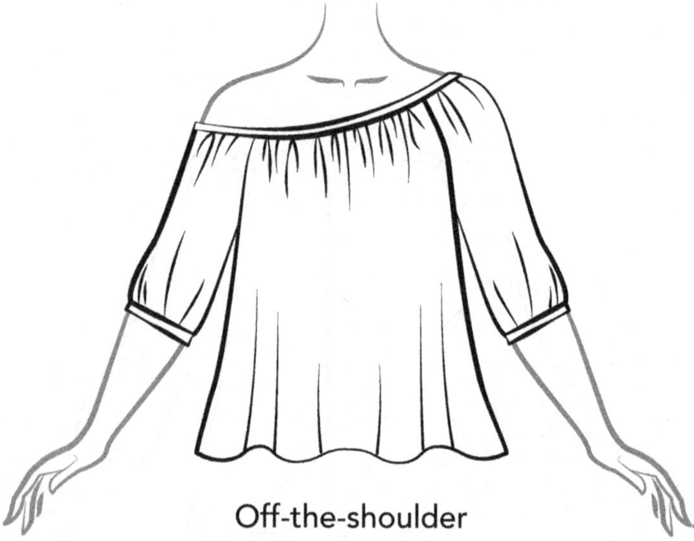

Off-the-shoulder

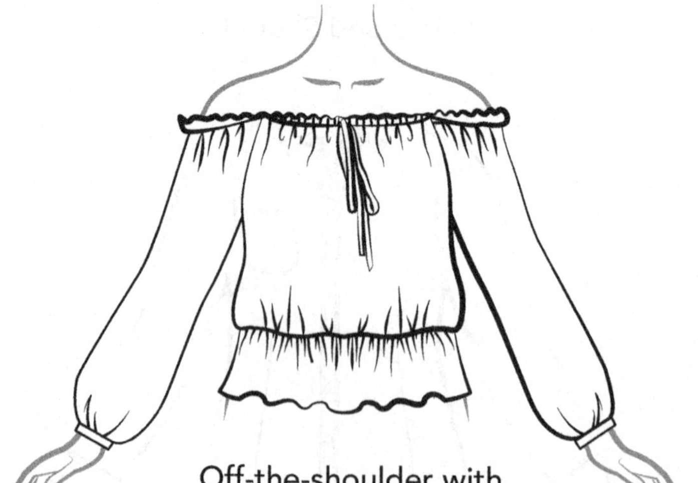

Off-the-shoulder with
Elasticated Waistline
(Peasant Blouse)

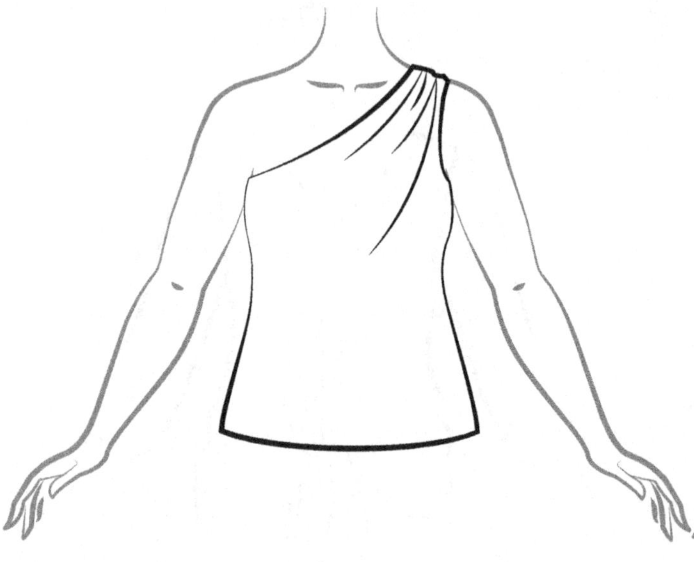

One-shoulder with Pleats
(Asymmetrical)

Overblouse

Styled Tops

Peplum Blouse - Halter

Prairie

Ruched
(Ballet Blouse)

Ruched with Midriff
and Sleeves

Sleeveless Shell

Smocked

Styled Tops

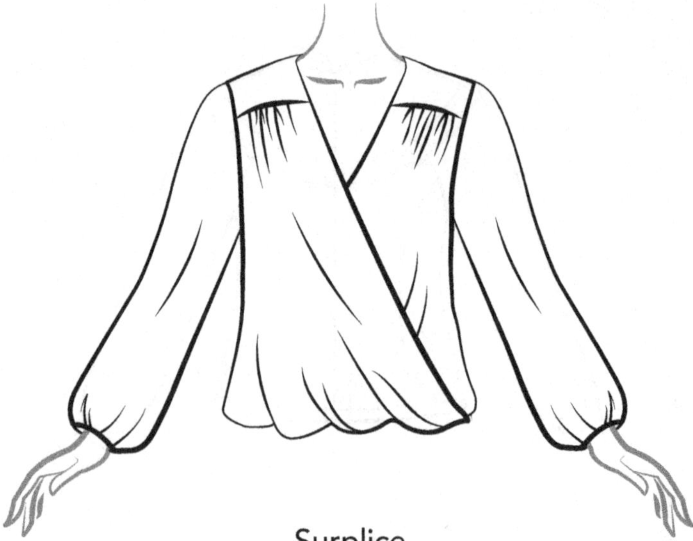

Surplice

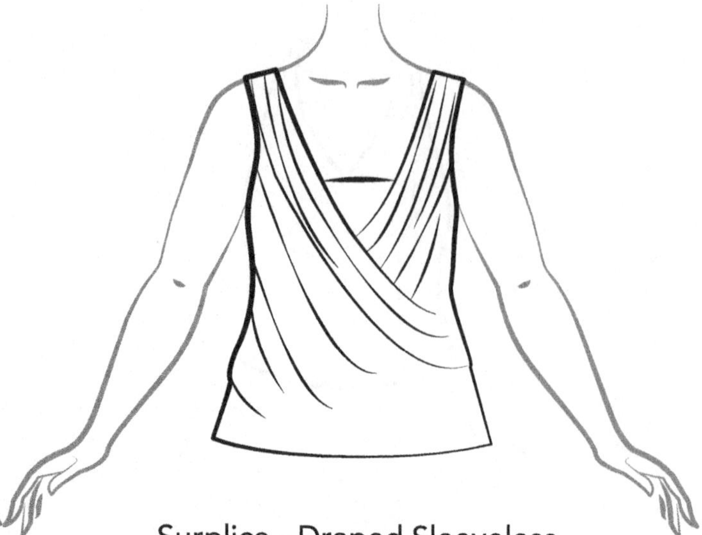

Surplice - Draped Sleeveless

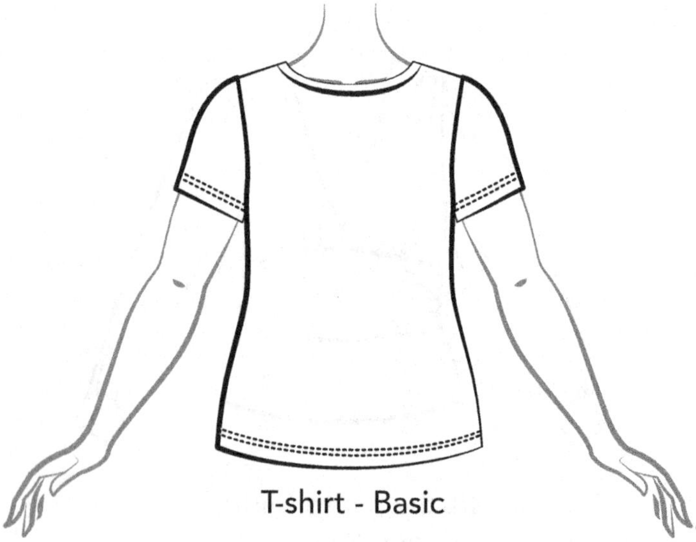

T-shirt - Basic

Tent Silhouette with a Yoke
and Puff Sleeves

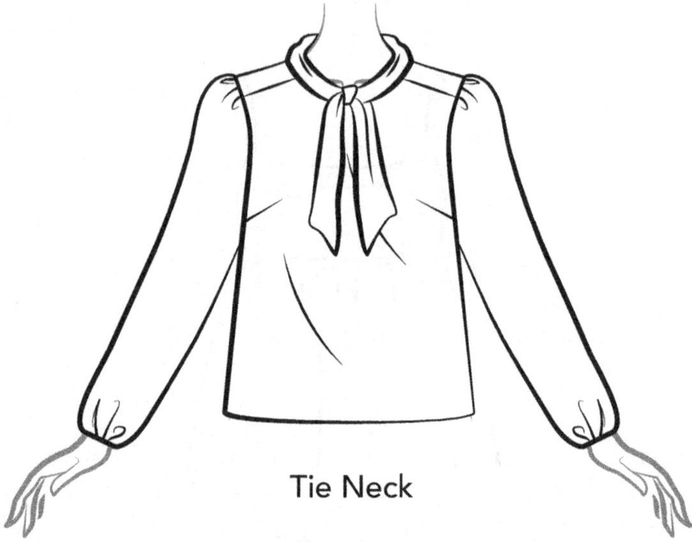

Tie Neck

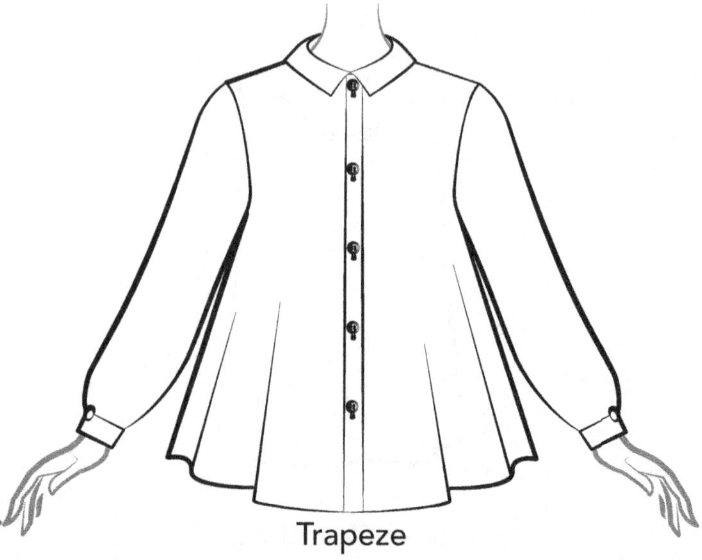

Trapeze

Styled Tops

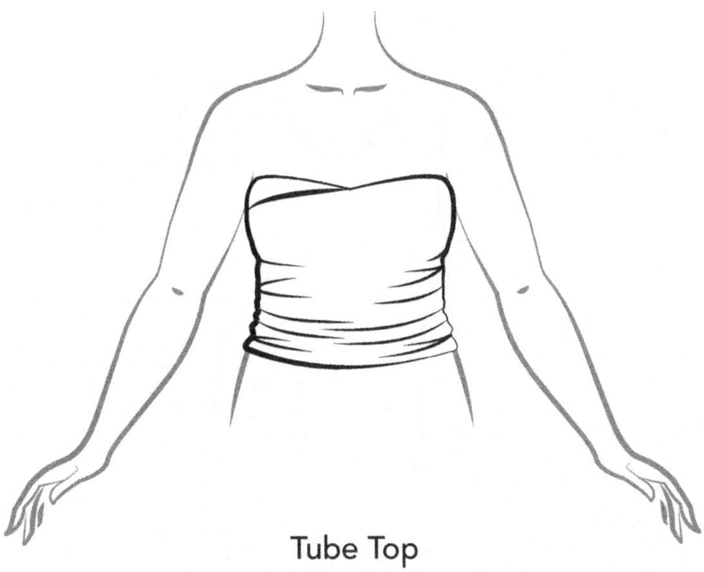

Tube Top

Tunic Length with a Dolman Sleeve

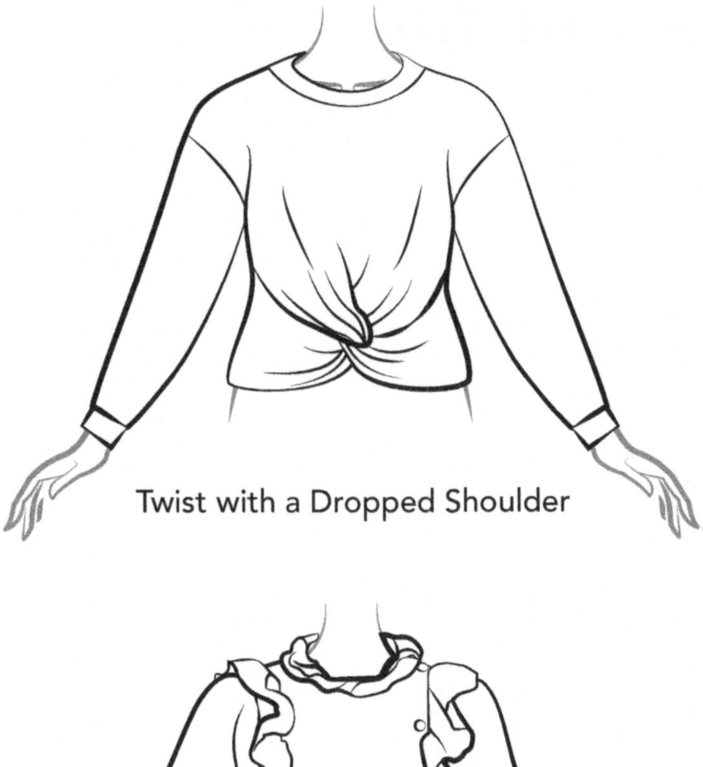

Twist with a Dropped Shoulder

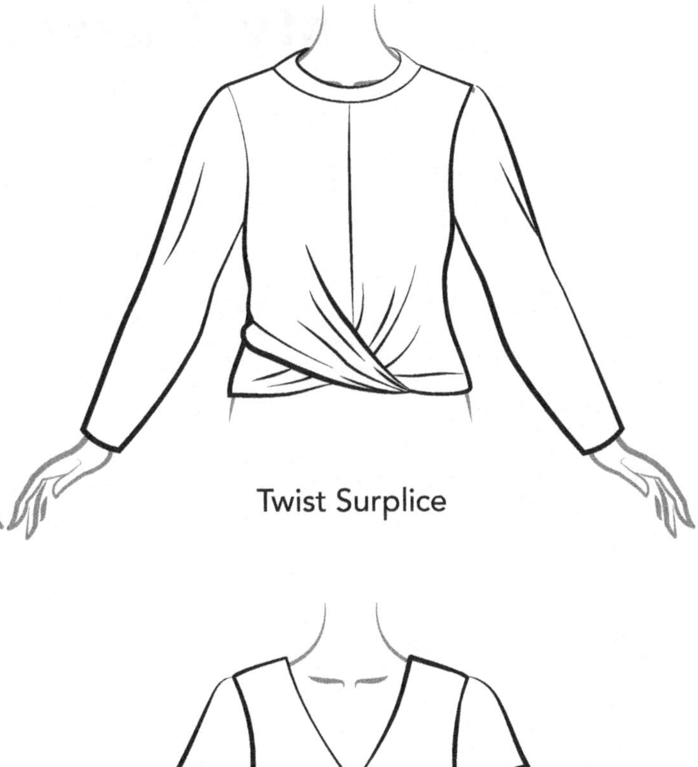

Twist Surplice

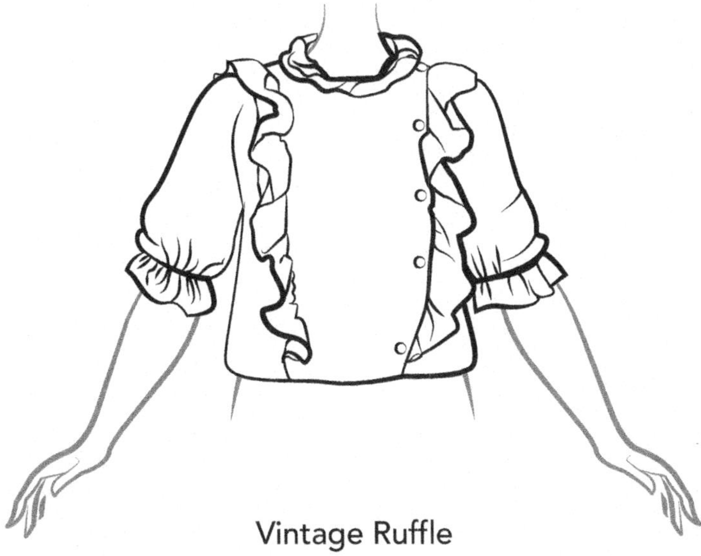

Vintage Ruffle

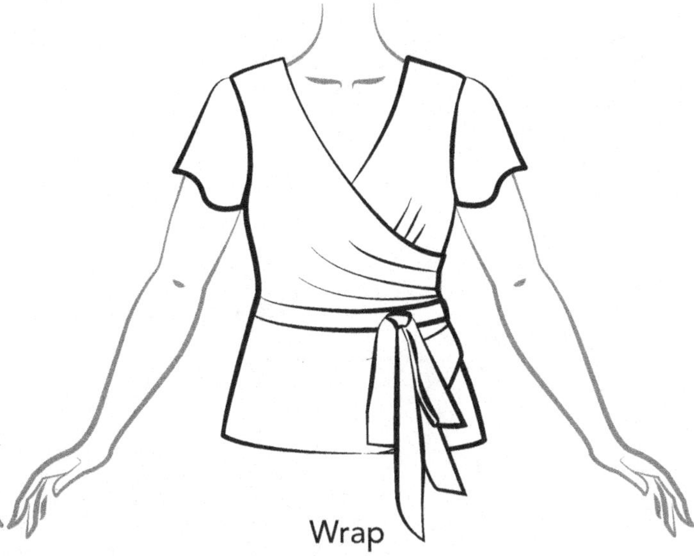

Wrap

Styled Tops

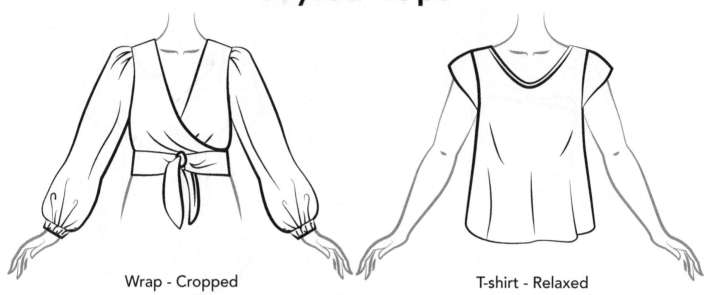

Wrap - Cropped

T-shirt - Relaxed

My Customized Tops

My Customized Tops

Cardigans, Pullovers, and Sweaters

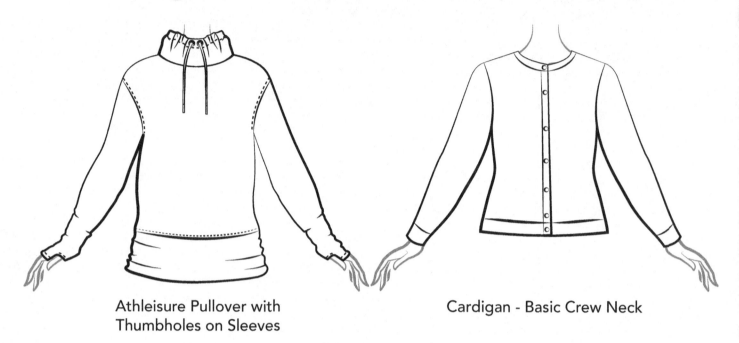

Athleisure Pullover with
Thumbholes on Sleeves

Cardigan - Basic Crew Neck

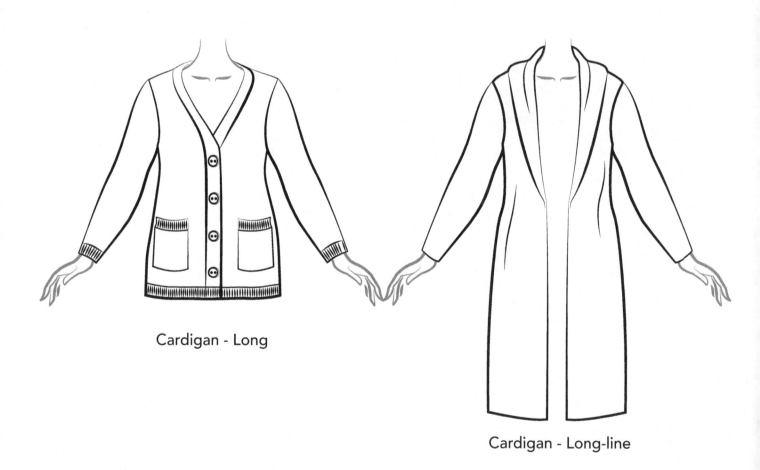

Cardigan - Long

Cardigan - Long-line

Cardigans, Pullovers, and Sweaters

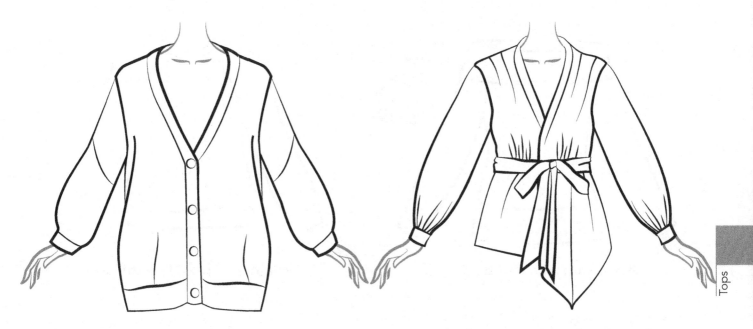

Cardigan - V-neck Slouchy

Cardigan - Wrap with a Tie Belt
and an Asymmetric Hemline

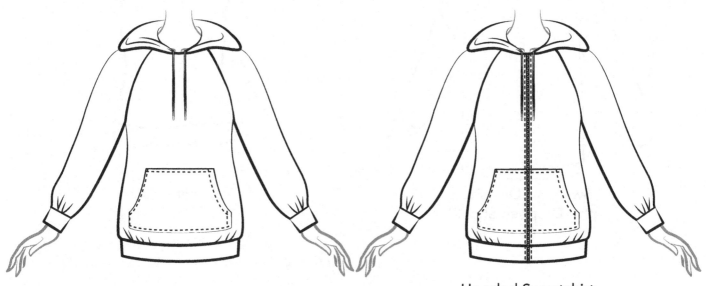

Hooded Sweatshirt - Pullover
(Hoodie)

Hooded Sweatshirt
with a Zipper
(Hoodie - Zippered)

Cardigans, Pullovers, and Sweaters

Sew this style!
Purchase the sewing pattern here:

Pullover with a Folded Boat Neck

Sweater - Crew Neck Pullover

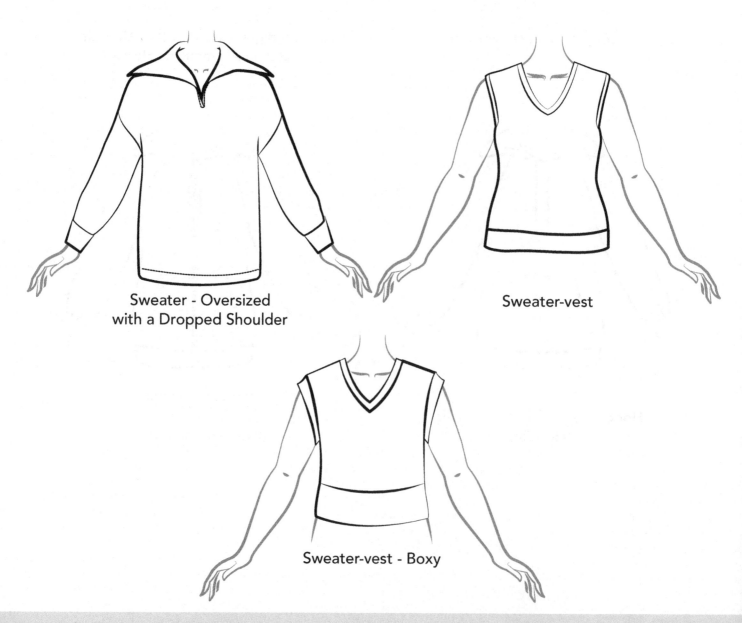

Sweater - Oversized
with a Dropped Shoulder

Sweater-vest

Sweater-vest - Boxy

My Customized Cardigans, Pullovers, and Sweaters

Tops

Blazers

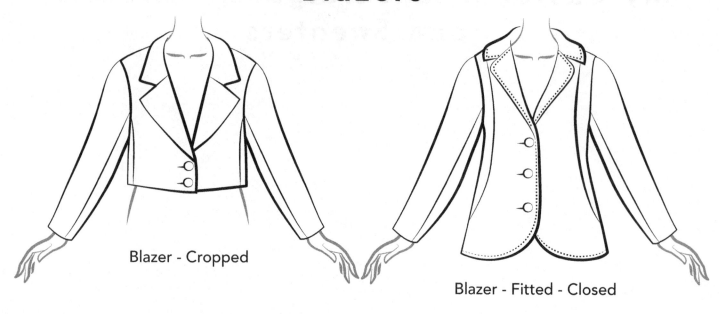

Blazer - Cropped

Blazer - Fitted - Closed

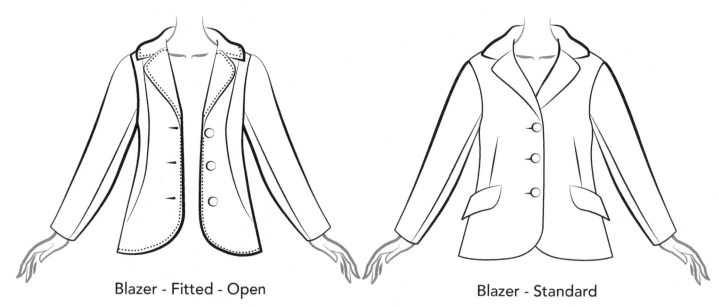

Blazer - Fitted - Open

Blazer - Standard

Blazer - Straight (Boxy)

Capes, Jackets, and Coats

A-line

Barrel

Biker (Mortorcycle)

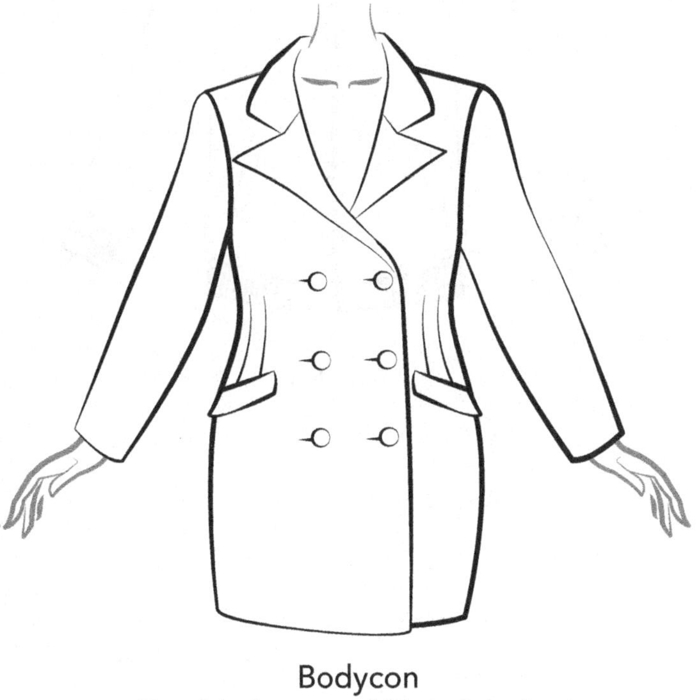

Bodycon
(Double-breasted Fitted Jacket)

Capes, Jackets, and Coats

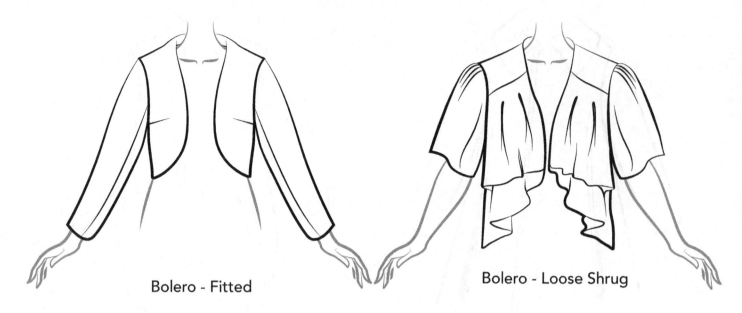

Bolero - Fitted

Bolero - Loose Shrug

Sew this style!
Purchase the sewing
pattern here:

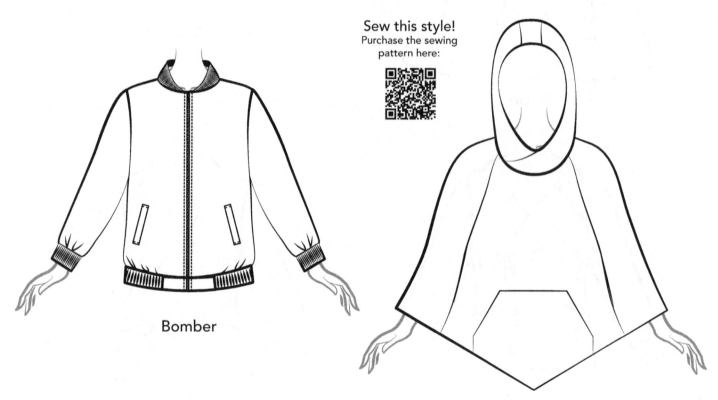

Bomber

Cape - Hooded

Capes, Jackets, and Coats

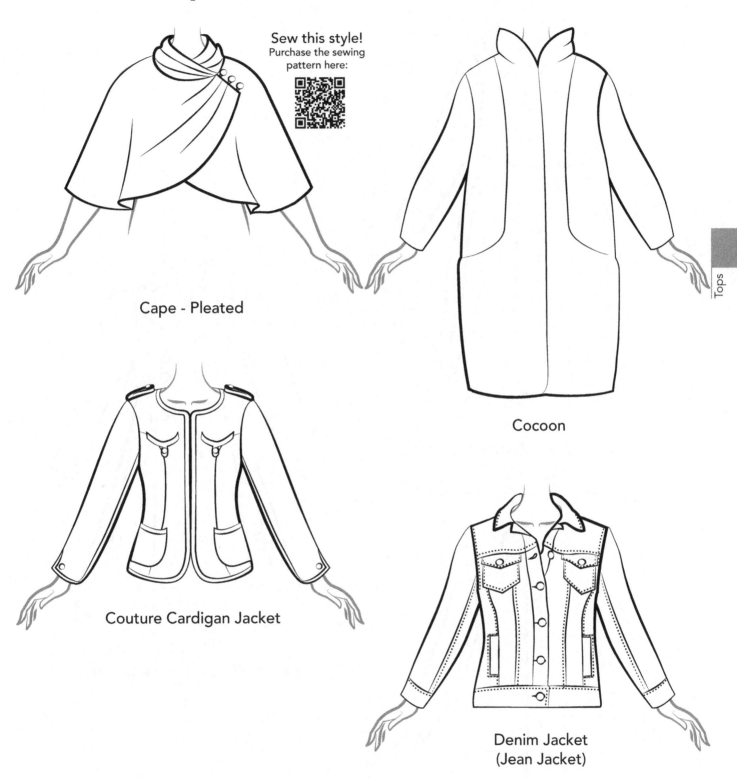

Sew this style!
Purchase the sewing
pattern here:

Cape - Pleated

Cocoon

Couture Cardigan Jacket

Denim Jacket
(Jean Jacket)

Capes, Jackets, and Coats

Fit and Flare - Bubble Hem

Fit and Flare - Double-breasted

Funnel Neck Fitted

Capes, Jackets, and Coats

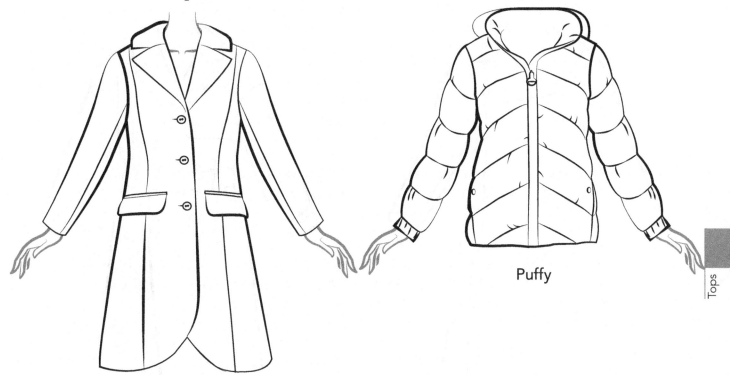

Long-line Blazer-inspired

Puffy

Puffy - Long-line

Raincoat

Capes, Jackets, and Coats

Straight-line - Double-breasted with an
Empire Waistline and Full Length

Trench

Varsity

Capes, Jackets, and Coats

Waterfall

Wrap-over
Hourglass Silhouette and a
Handkerchief Hem

My Customized Blazers, Capes, Jackets, and Coats

My Customized Blazers, Capes, Jackets, and Coats

Dresses

The dresses in this chapter are basic and showcase common silhouettes for high-fashion and everyday occasions.

Certain silhouettes look exceptionally good on specific body types. Some silhouettes may not be as flattering as others based on the body type. You may already know some of your favorite silhouettes. I recommend studying your favorites among the clothes you own.

To study this topic in-depth, I recommend taking an online course I teach called "Define, Design, & Love Your Style." The course delves into designing for specific body types and curating your (or your client's) dream collection. This allows you to find clothes you love every time you look in your closet.

To learn more about the online course "Define, Design, & Love Your Style," scan this QR code and sign up for the waitlist:

A quick tip: As you design, an important question is, "How does the person put on the garment? Is there a zipper or button closure, and where is it (if it is not obvious in the image)?" You would be amazed by the number of designs I have seen over the years in which the designer does not consider how the wearer will put on the garment.

To learn more about this critical topic that designers often overlook, scan this QR code to watch a video:

It is time to dream up those beautiful dress styles and sketch them!

Dress Waistline and Length Options

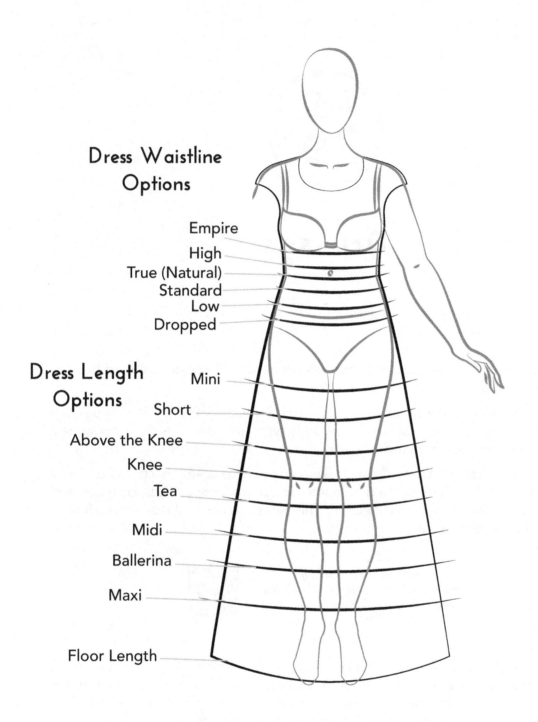

Dress Waistline Options

Empire
High
True (Natural)
Standard
Low
Dropped

Dress Length Options

Mini
Short
Above the Knee
Knee
Tea
Midi
Ballerina
Maxi
Floor Length

Dresses

A-line

Apron (Pinafore)

Dresses

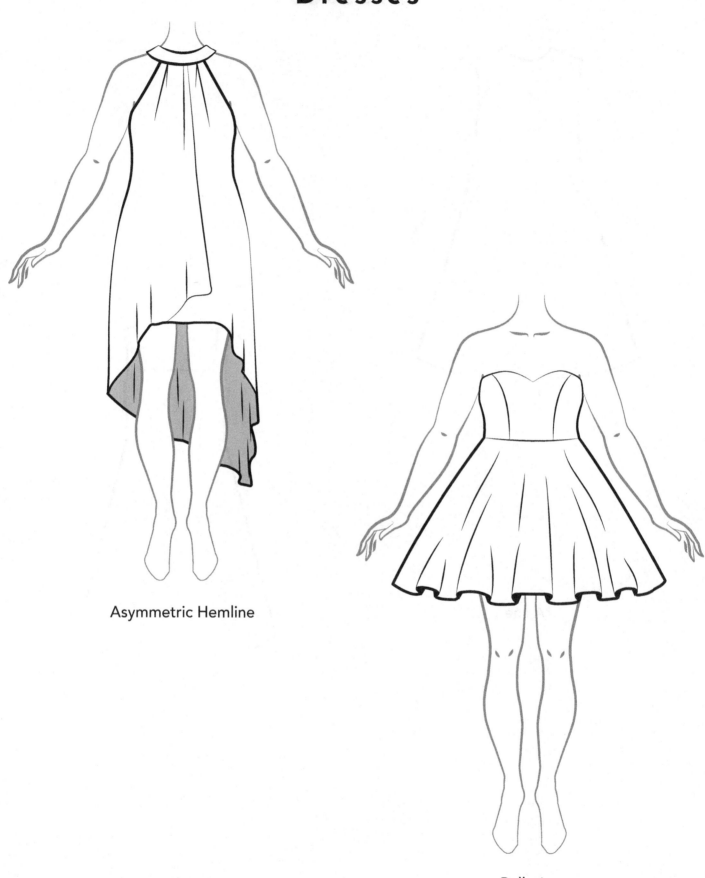

Asymmetric Hemline

Ballerina

Dresses

Ballgown (Princess Gown)

Dresses

Ballgown with Princess Seams and a Train

Dresses

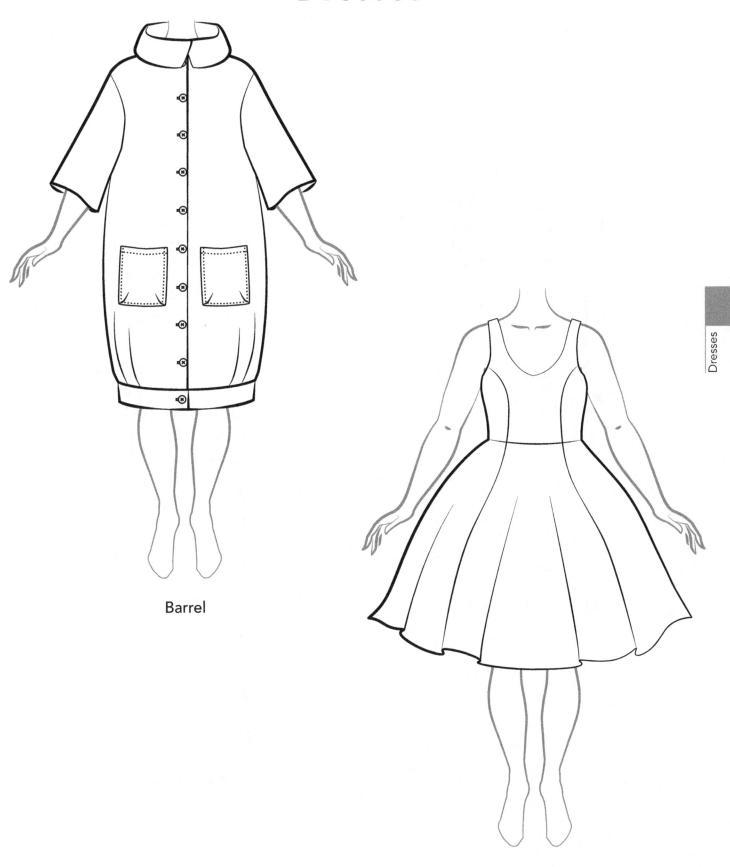

Barrel

Bell (Fit and Flare)

Dresses

Blouson - Low Waist

Blouson - True Waist

Dresses

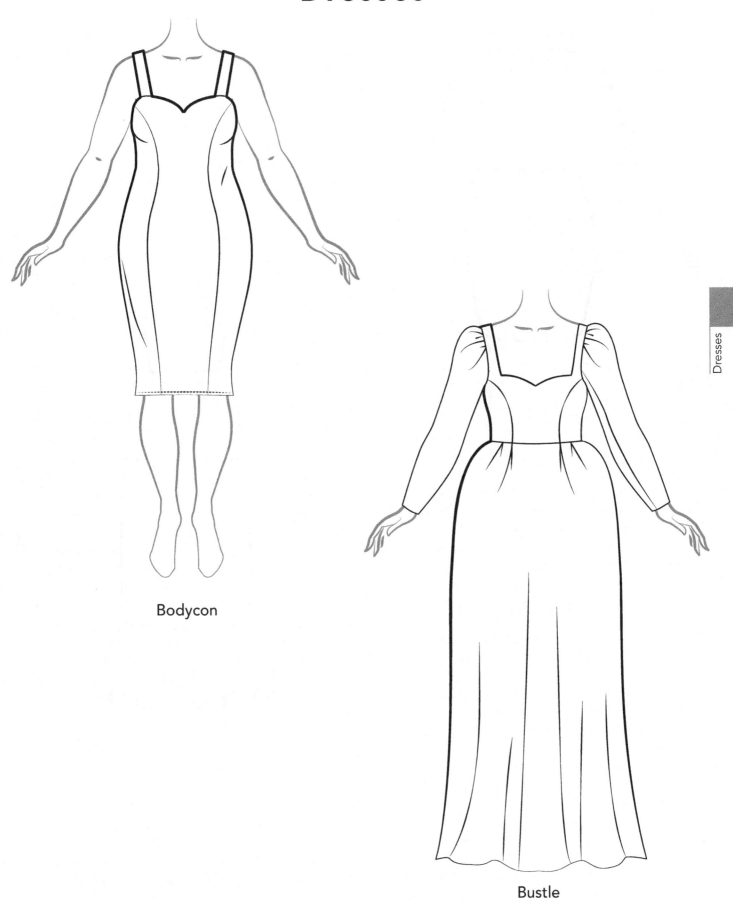

Bodycon

Bustle

Dresses

Cape Dress

Charleston

Dresses

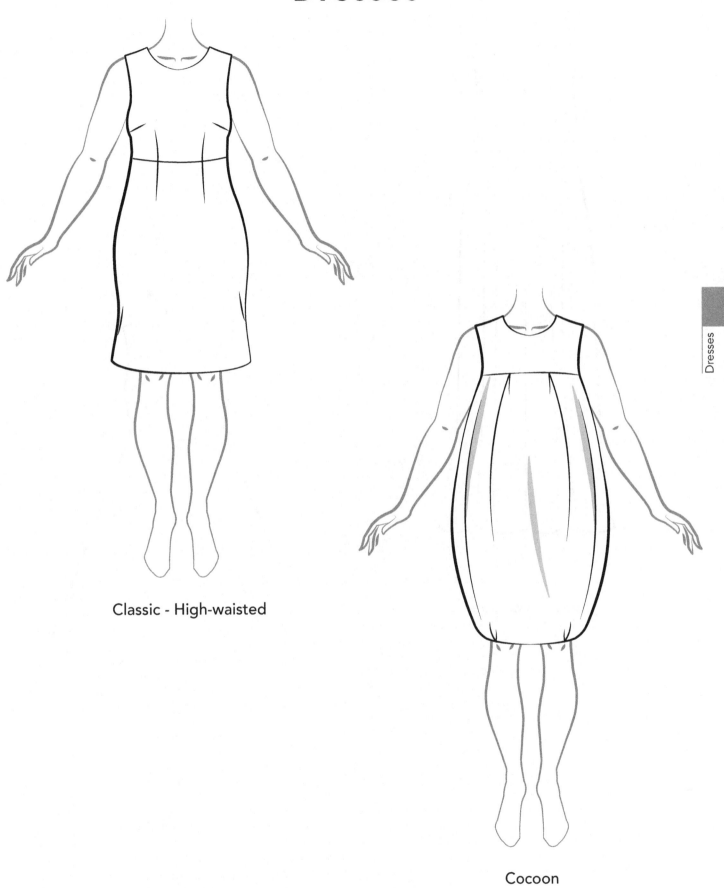

Classic - High-waisted

Cocoon

Dresses

Empire Waistline

Fit and Flare (X-line)

Dresses

Sew this style!
Purchase the sewing pattern here:

Fit and Flare with
Soft Fullness

Flapper - Dropped Waist and
Straight-line

Dresses

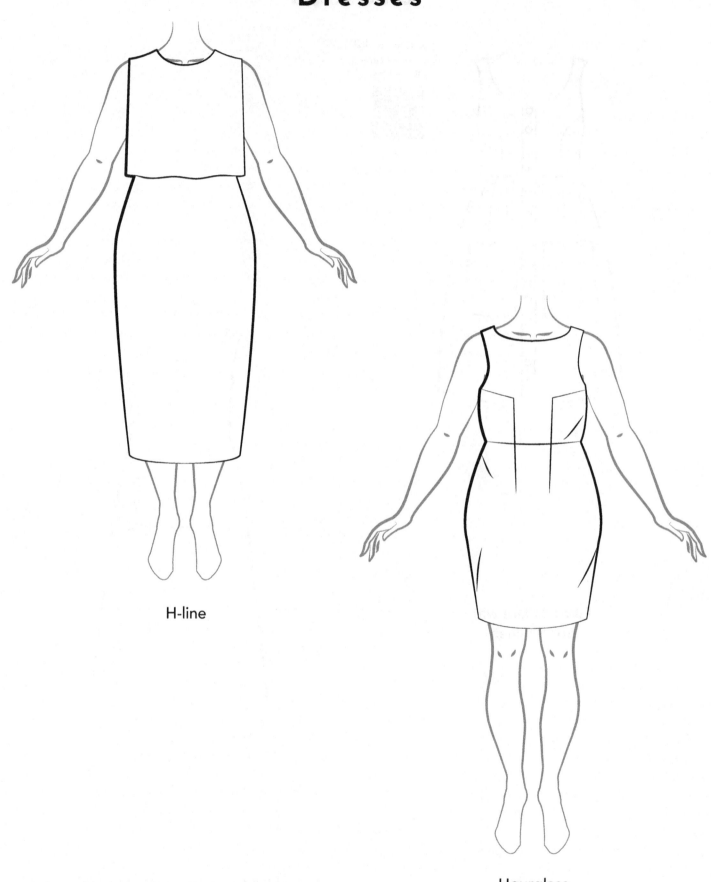

H-line

Hourglass

Dresses

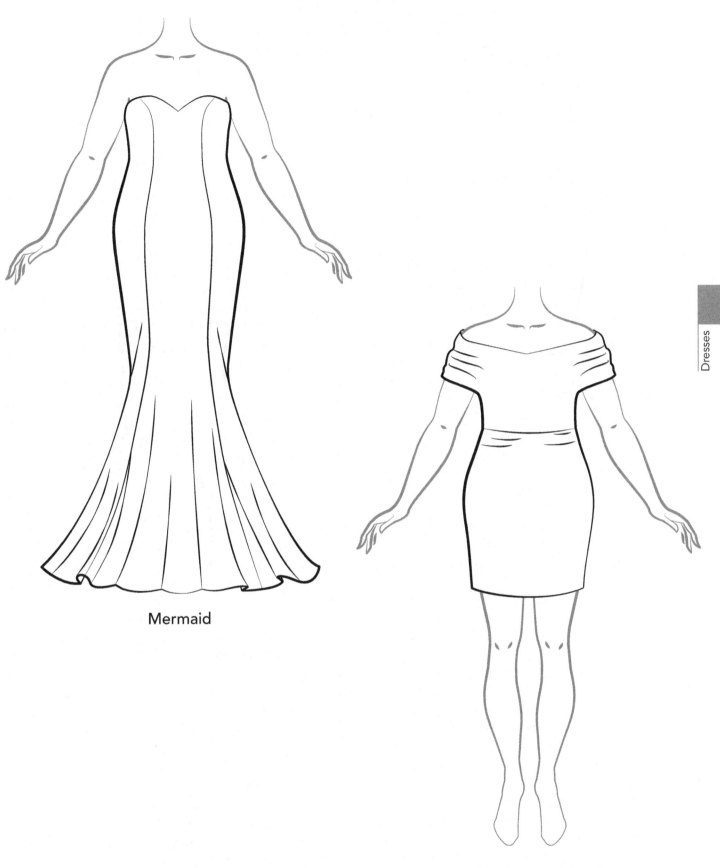

Mermaid

Off-the-shoulder

Dresses

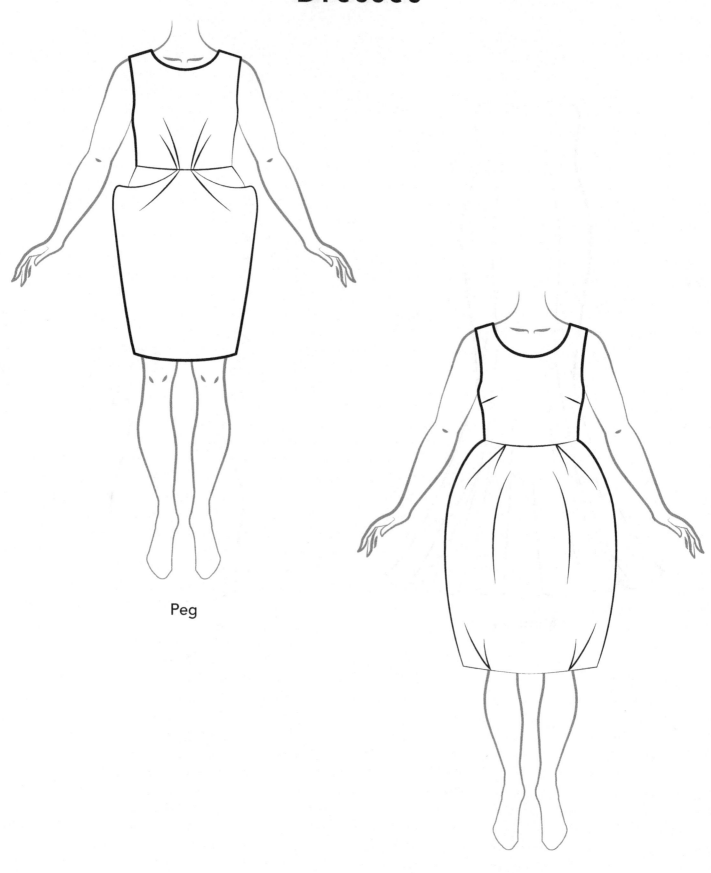

Peg

Pouf (Balloon)

Dresses

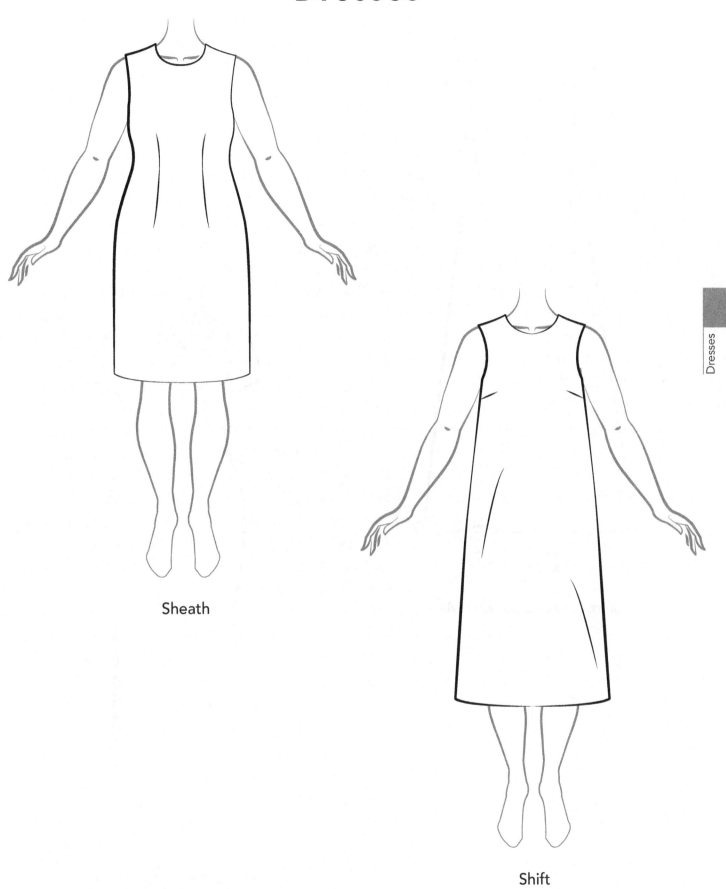

Sheath

Shift

Dresses

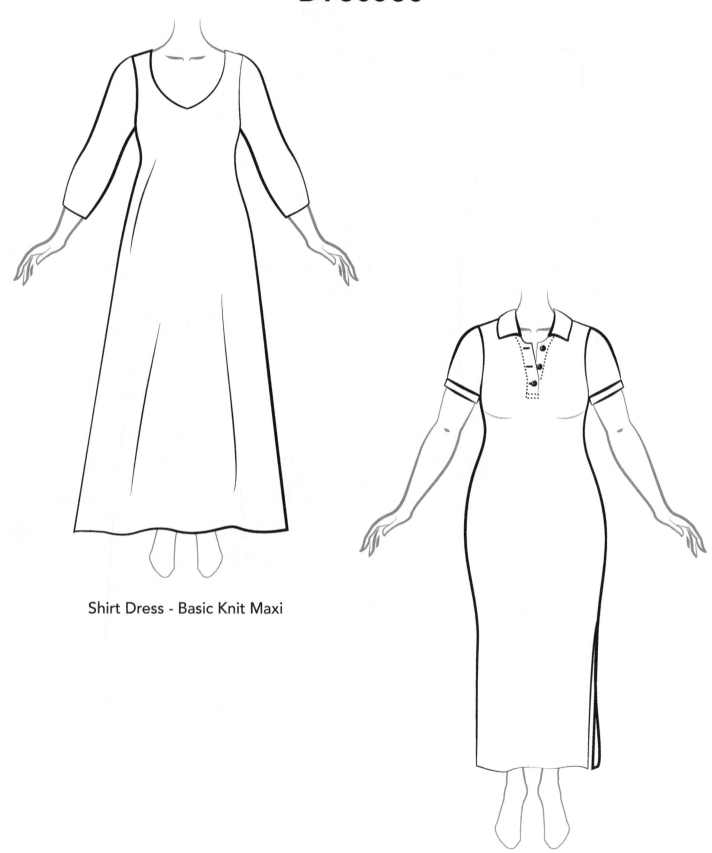

Shirt Dress - Basic Knit Maxi

Shirt Dress - Polo Collar
and Maxi Length

Dresses

Shirt Dress - Woven

Slip Dress

Dresses

Tent (Trapeze)

Tiered

Dresses

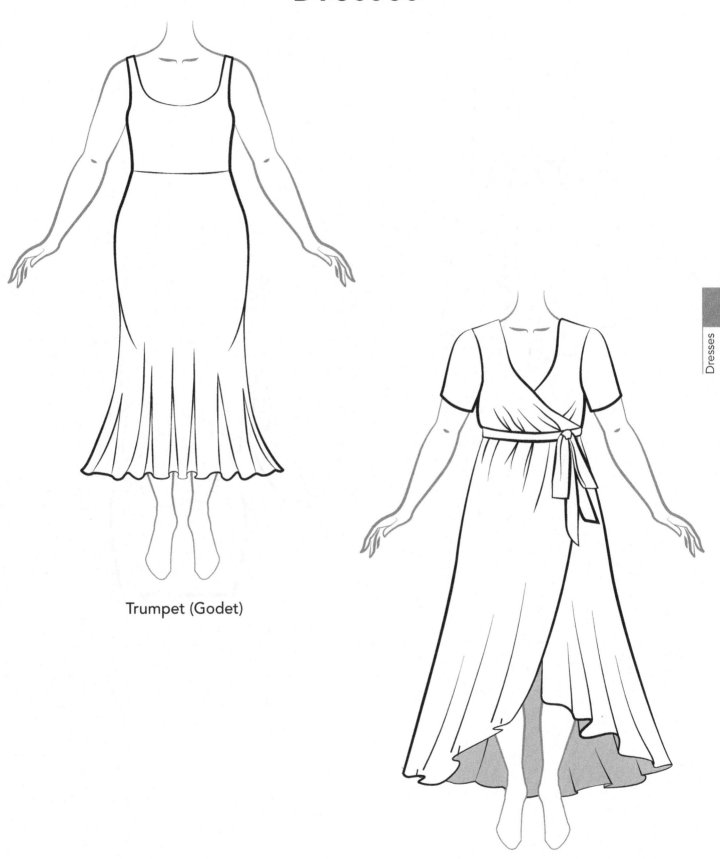

Trumpet (Godet)

Wrap - Maxi Length

Dresses

Wrap

Y-line - Dolman Sleeve with an
Oversized Top and a Tight Skirt

Dresses

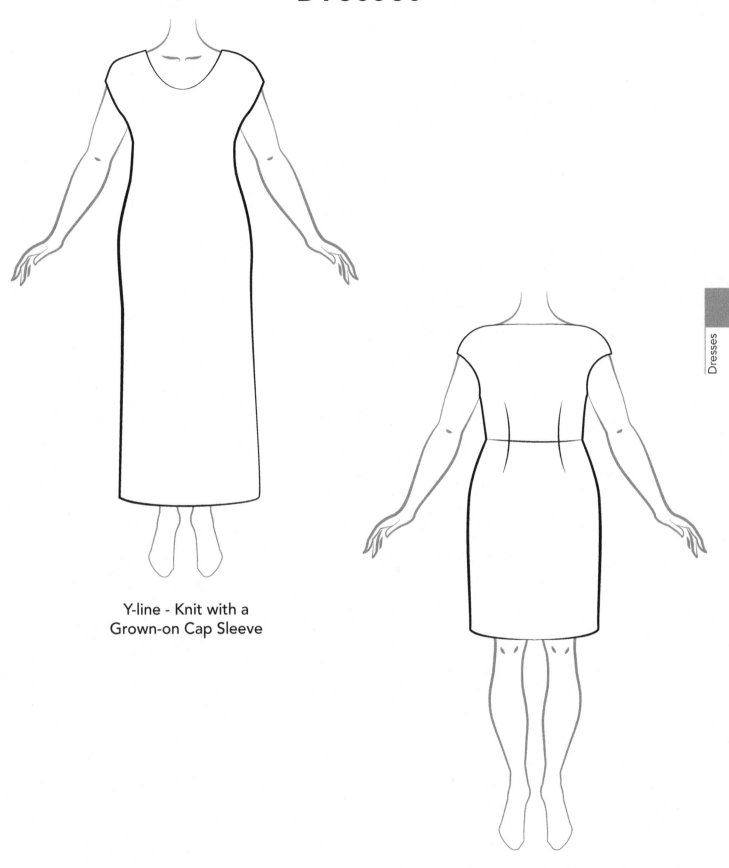

Y-line - Knit with a
Grown-on Cap Sleeve

Y-line - Woven with a
Grown-on Cap Sleeve

My Customized Dresses

Skirts

Skirts are so fun to draw, especially when you use them to create new dress silhouettes. Mix and match these skirts with the top/bodice silhouettes to create your styles (see pages 52-54 and 64-74 for the top/bodice silhouettes). Change the length and fullness of the skirt to demonstrate how you envision the design.

The fullness of a skirt has two factors:

1) The fabric selected;

2) The shape of the sewing pattern.

Refer to page 17 to see how the fabric drape and shape of the pattern affect a circle skirt.

To see a free video that explains this topic more, scan this QR code:

Skirt Waistline and Length Options

Skirt Waistline Options

- High
- True (or) Natural
- Standard
- Low

Skirt Length Options

- Micro
- Mini
- Short
- Above the Knee
- Knee
- Tea
- Midi
- Ballerina
- Maxi
- Floor

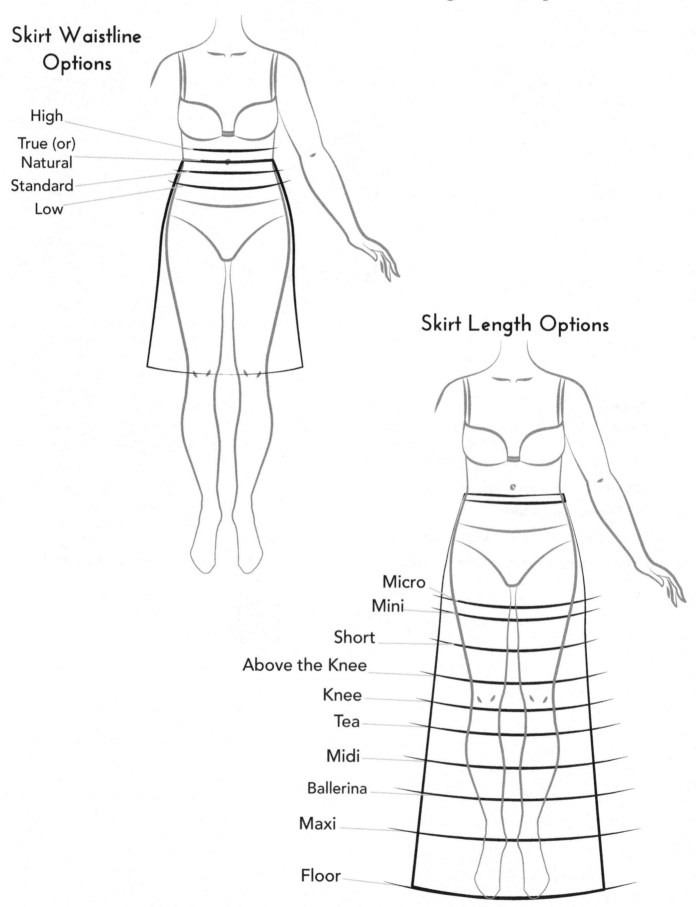

Skirts

A-line

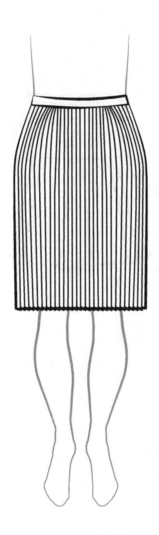

Accordion Pleated

Asymmetrical

Skirts

Bell

Box Pleat with a Knife
Edge and an A-line
Flare

Bubble

Skirts

Buttoned Straight

Circle Skirt
Average-drape Fabric

Circle Skirt
Full-drape Fabric
See the Ruffle Section for
additional options.

Circle Skirt
Soft-drape Flowing Fabric

Skirts

Cowl Drape

Dirndl Skirt

Draped

Skirts

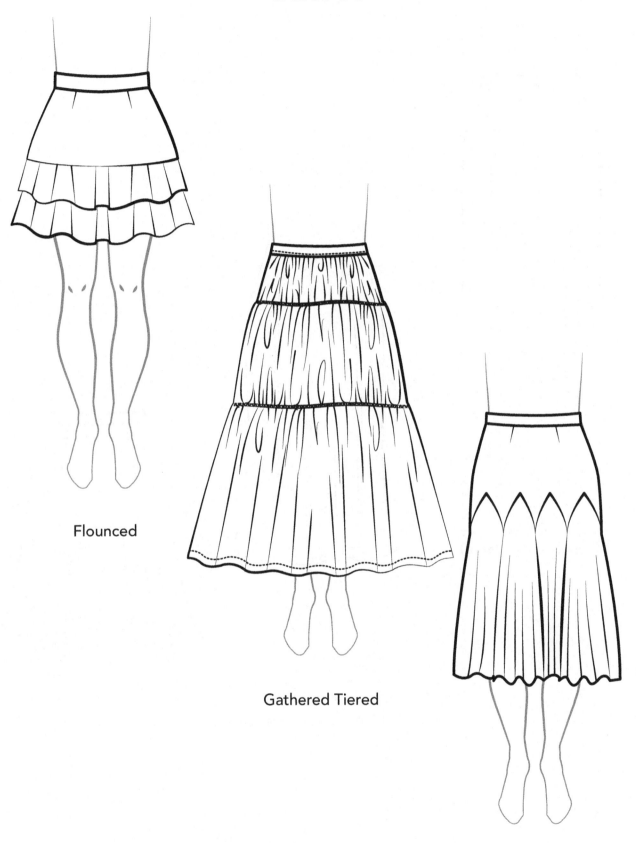

Flounced

Gathered Tiered

Godet Panel

Skirts

Gored
(Panelled or 6-Gore)

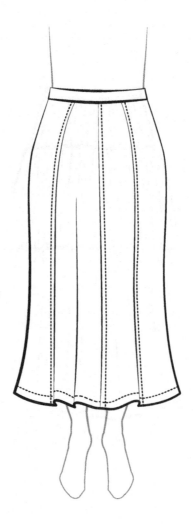

Gored
(Panelled or 8-Gore)

Hankerchief

Skirts

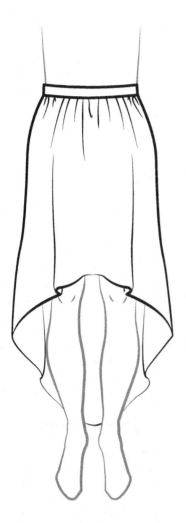

High-low

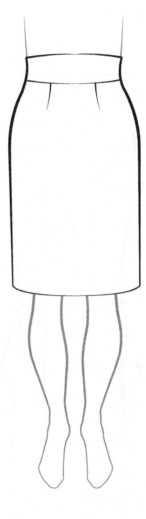

High-waisted

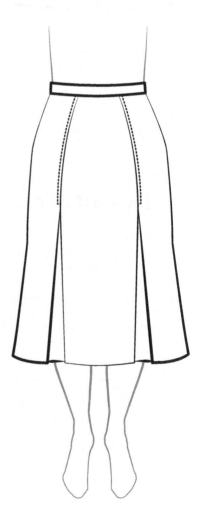

Kick-pleat

Skirts

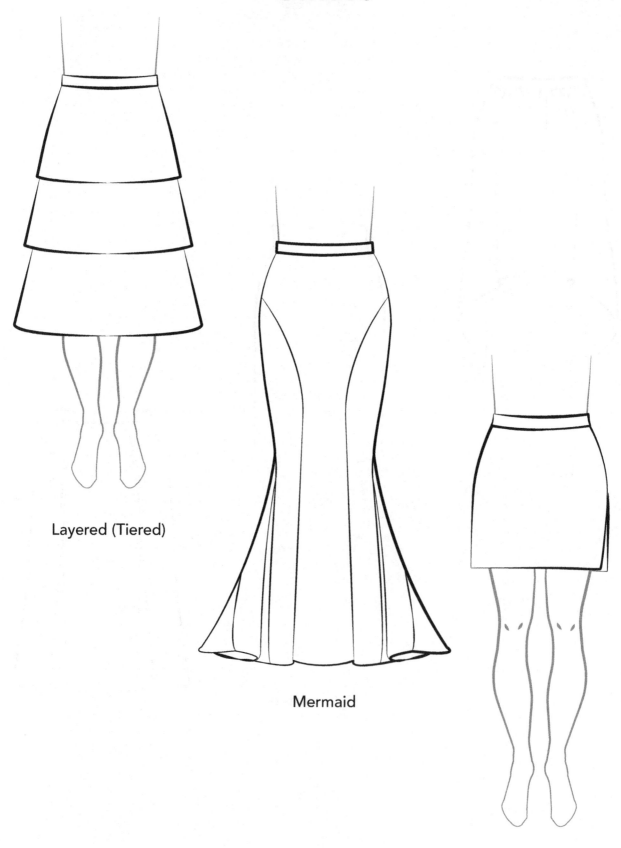

Layered (Tiered)

Mermaid

Mini

Skirts

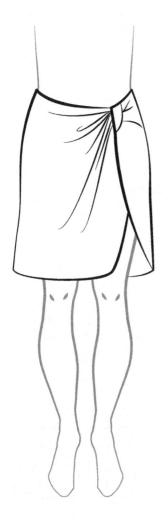

Pareo

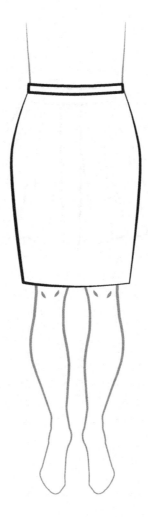

Pencil
This must have a vent
at the side seam or on
the center back seam.

Peplum Skirt

Skirts

Pleated with Inverted Pleats

Rah-rah
(Cheerleader)

Ruffled Tiered

Skirts

Sheath
with a Slit

Side Pleat

Skort

Skirts

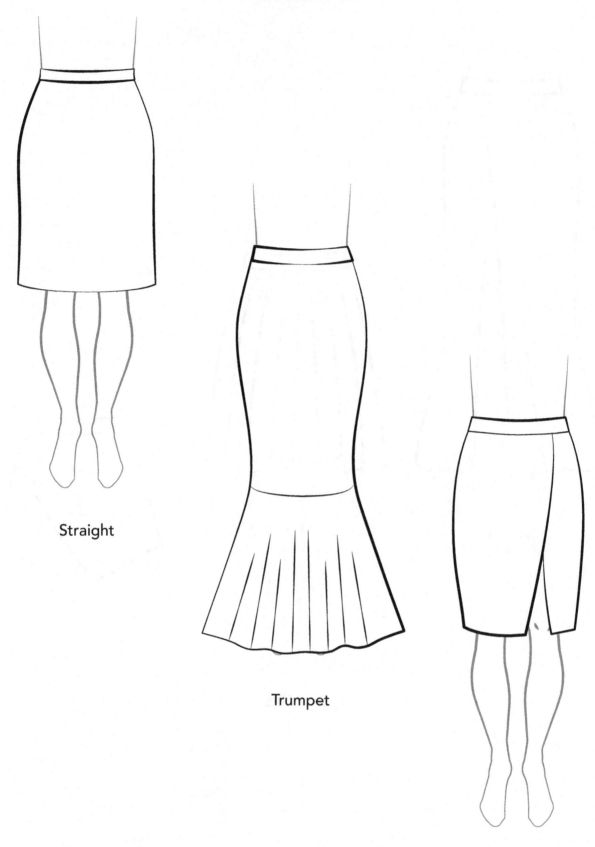

Straight

Trumpet

Tulip

Skirts

Wrap

Yoke with Directional
Side Pleats

My Customized Skirts

Pants, Shorts, Jumpsuits, Overalls, and Rompers

The silhouettes of pants (or trousers if you are from the UK) are ever-changing. The library of silhouettes in this chapter also includes many design details from which you can choose. Additionally, this chapter includes jeans, shorts, jumpsuits, overalls, and rompers.

In later chapters, there are many more pockets, waistbands, and other design details. Once again, change or add design details to create your new styles.

To see an example of a mix-and-match creation for pants, scan this QR code:

Create your own one-piece outfits by combining the pants silhouettes from this chapter with the tops and sleeves chapters earlier in the book.

Don't forget to check the Video Vault for more options. By now, you should have signed up for the Free Video Vault and saved the page in your favorites on your computer so you can return to it as you design.

To gain access to the free Video Vault, scan this QR code:

Pants Waistline and Length Options

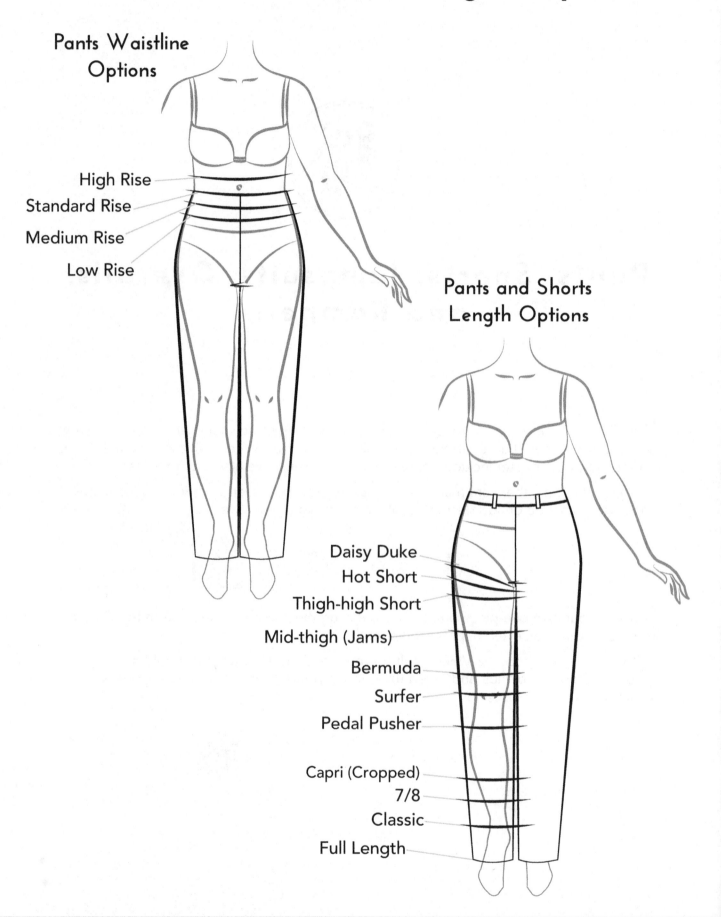

Pants Waistline Options

- High Rise
- Standard Rise
- Medium Rise
- Low Rise

Pants and Shorts Length Options

- Daisy Duke
- Hot Short
- Thigh-high Short
- Mid-thigh (Jams)
- Bermuda
- Surfer
- Pedal Pusher
- Capri (Cropped)
- 7/8
- Classic
- Full Length

Pants (Trousers)

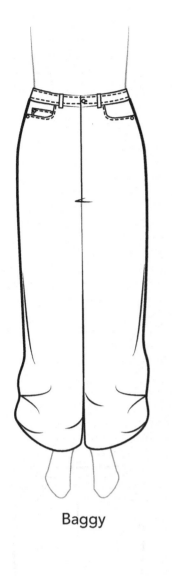

Baggy

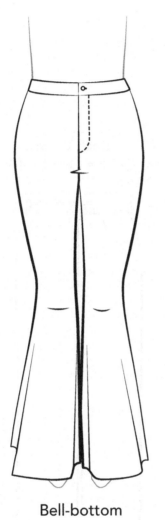

Bell-bottom

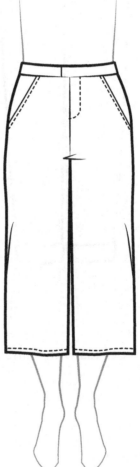
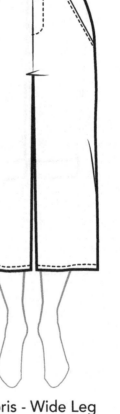

Capris - Wide Leg

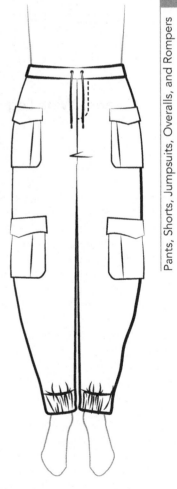

Cargos - Narrowed Leg
(Carrot)

Pants

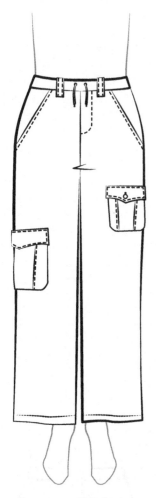

Cargos - Wide Leg

Chinos with Cuffs

Back View:
Chinos - No Cuffs

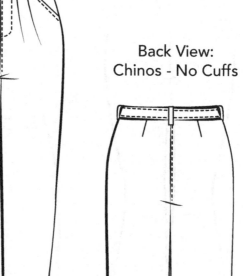

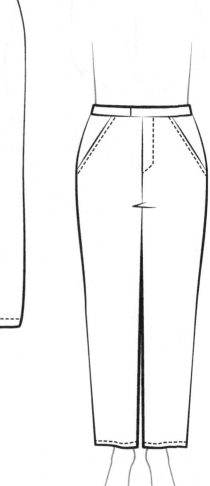

Cigarette
(Carrot)

Pants

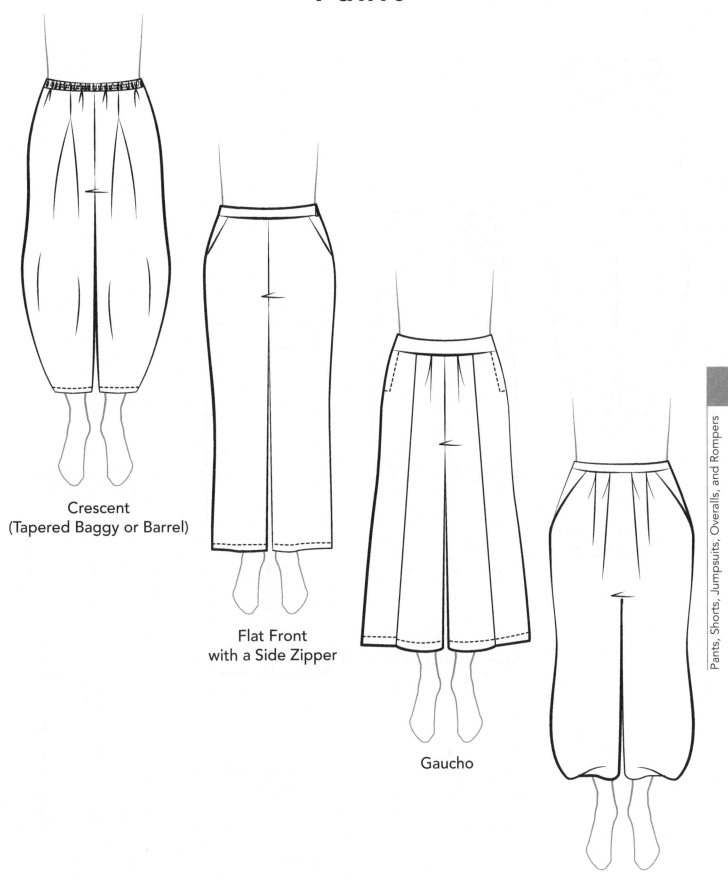

Crescent
(Tapered Baggy or Barrel)

Flat Front
with a Side Zipper

Gaucho

Harem
(Zouave, Sarouel, or Aladdin)

Pants

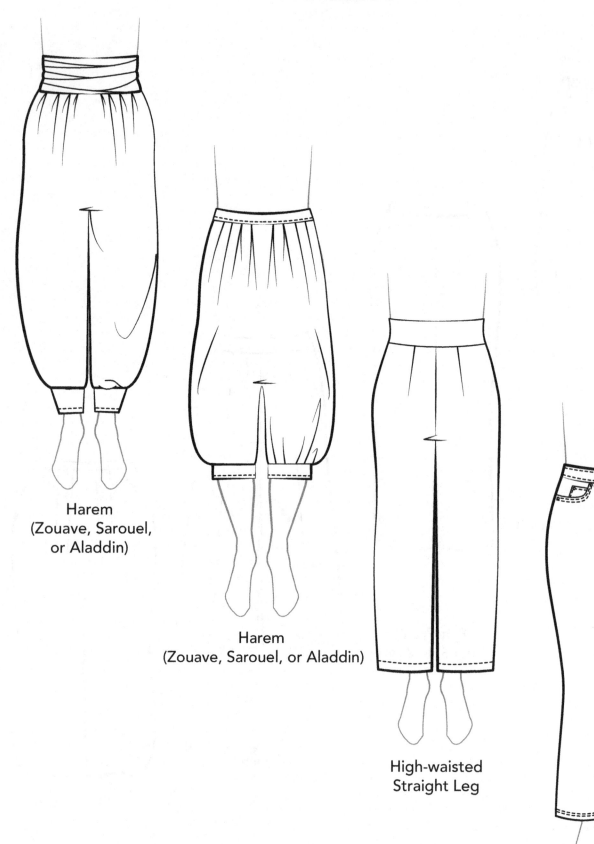

Harem
(Zouave, Sarouel,
or Aladdin)

Harem
(Zouave, Sarouel, or Aladdin)

High-waisted
Straight Leg

Jeans - Boot Cut

Pants

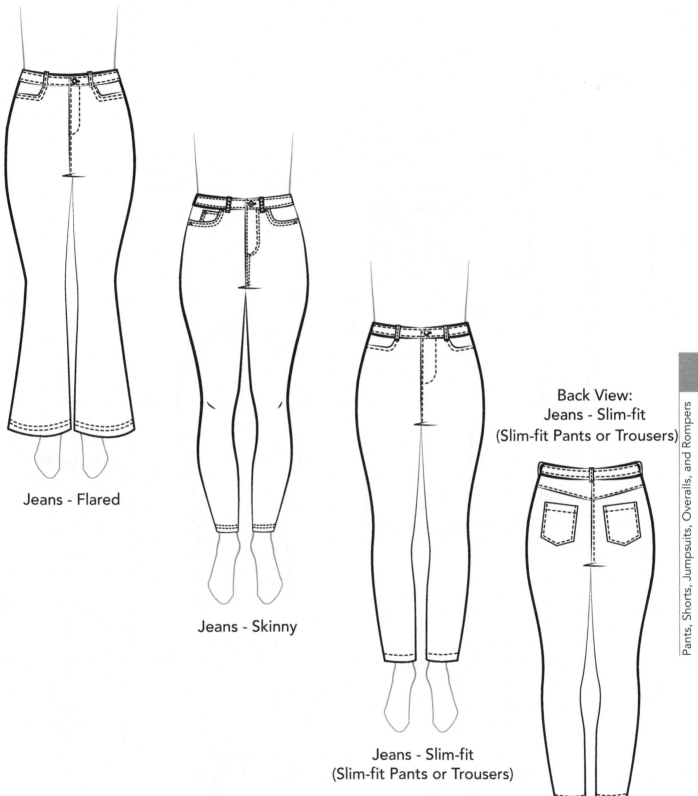

Jeans - Flared

Jeans - Skinny

Jeans - Slim-fit
(Slim-fit Pants or Trousers)

Back View:
Jeans - Slim-fit
(Slim-fit Pants or Trousers)

Pants

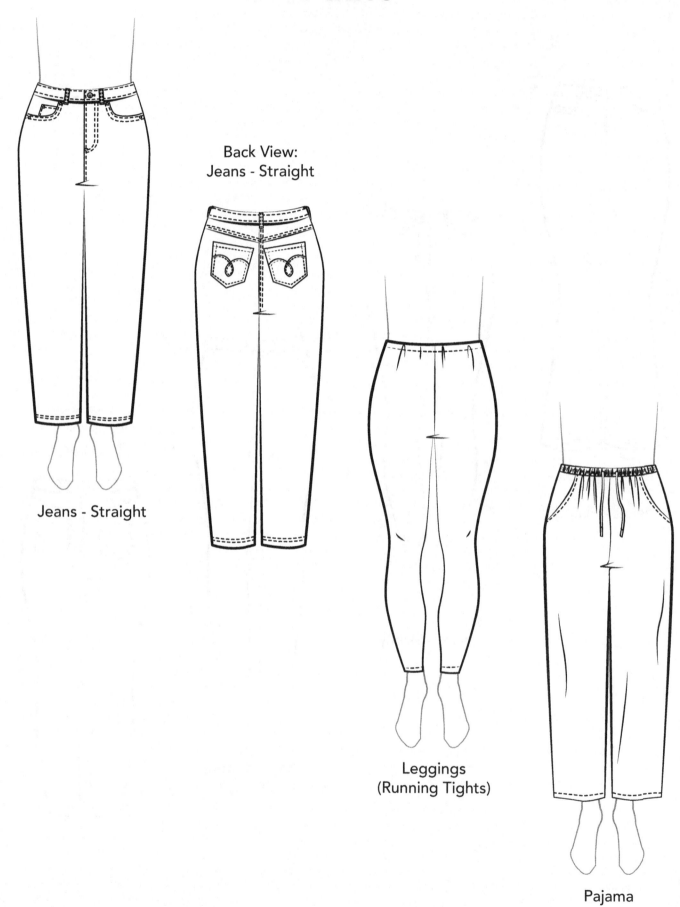

Back View:
Jeans - Straight

Jeans - Straight

Leggings
(Running Tights)

Pajama

Pants

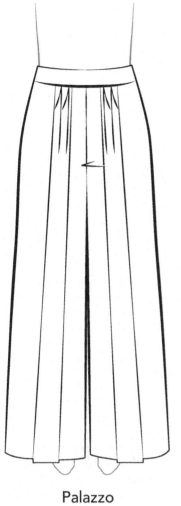

Palazzo

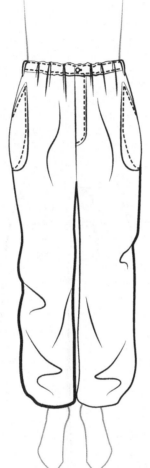

Parachute Pants

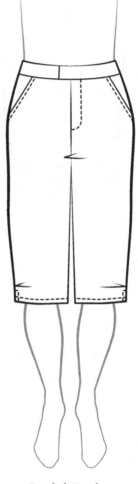

Pedal Pusher

Peplum Pants

Pants

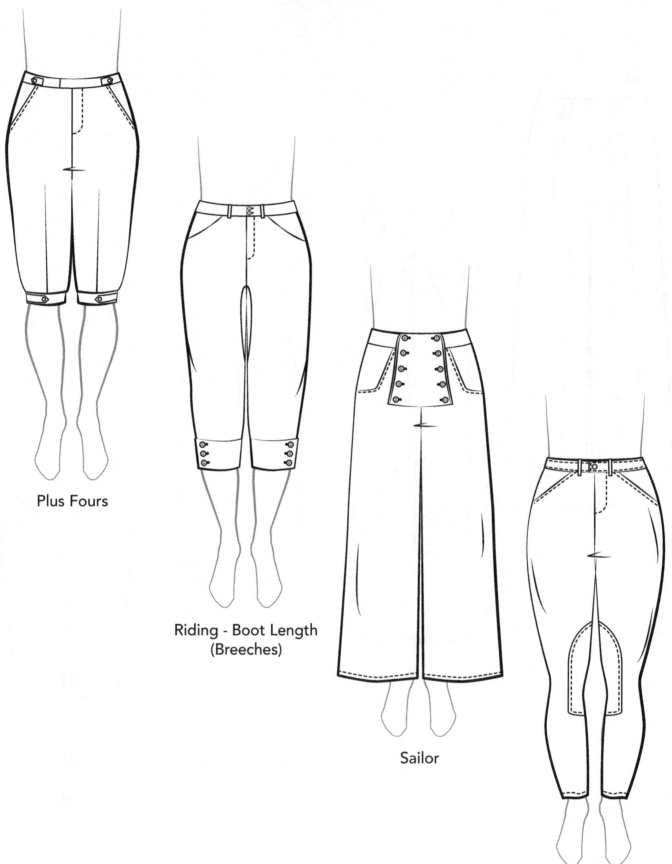

Plus Fours

Riding - Boot Length
(Breeches)

Sailor

Riding - Full-length
(Jodhpurs - Classic)

Pants

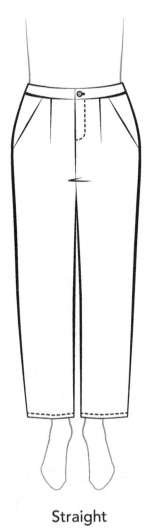

Straight

Back View:
Straight

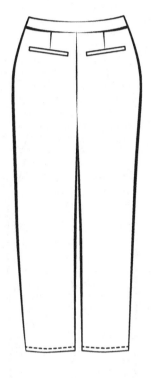

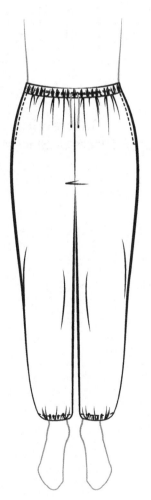

Surfer

Sweatpants (Joggers)

Pants

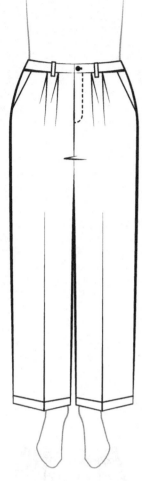

Tailored
(Trousers or Slacks)

Back View:
Tailored
(Trousers or Slacks)

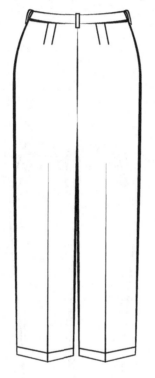

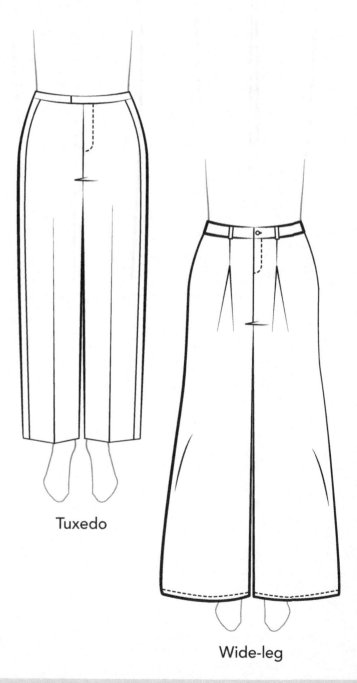

Tuxedo

Wide-leg

Pants

Yoked and
7/8 Length

Shorts

Shorts

Shorts - Bermuda

Shorts - Bloomers

Shorts - Hot

Shorts

My Customized Shorts

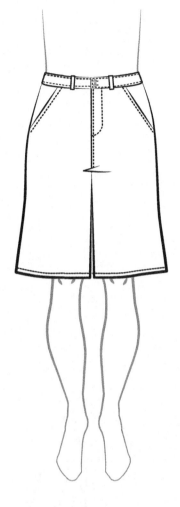

Shorts - Loose
and Knee Length

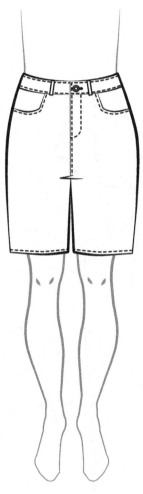

Shorts - Preppy

Jumpsuits

Jumpsuit - 3/4 Length

Jumpsuit - Surplice Front

Jumpsuit - Utility Style

Overalls and Rompers

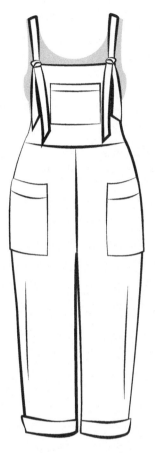

Overalls - Modern
(Coveralls)

Romper - Flowing
(Playsuit)

Romper - Surplice Front
(Playsuit)

My Customized Jumpsuits and Rompers

Pockets, Waistbands, and Other Design Details

Do you love styles with pockets? So many people love pockets. Throughout this chapter, there are many pockets to inspire you. Although several pockets might be specific to pants, most can also be added to tops, skirts, dresses, blazers, jackets, and coats.

Pockets do not need to be symmetrical, and you can place them in different locations. Examples: Have a single pocket on the leg of a pair of pants or the upper portion of a shirt or jacket.

If you want symmetry in your style, there are many pairs to select from for both the right and left sides of the garment.

To see an example of using pockets on multiple styles, scan this QR code:

If there is stitching on the pocket as a design detail, it is often symmetrical or mirrored from one pocket to the other. Alternatively, the topstitching design can continue from one pocket to the next, requiring multiple pockets to create the overall artwork.

Do you want any other topstitching on other seams? Often, these small design details like topstitching can dramatically change the aesthetic, especially when there is a contrasting thread color. Do not overlook the details. Many modern sewing machines have settings that make beautiful stitched designs. Design your own stitching and shapes for your signature look.

This chapter also showcases different waistbands, belts, buckles, and other common trims. Sometimes, these small design details can really change the aesthetic of the garment, making it stand out from other garments.

Patch Pockets

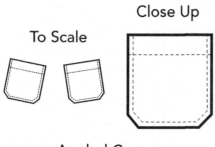

Close Up

To Scale

Angled Corners

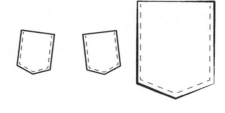

Angled Patch

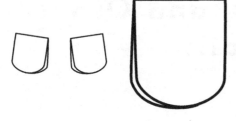

Bellow Rounded

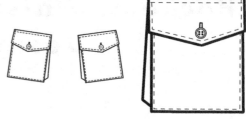

Bellow Cargo

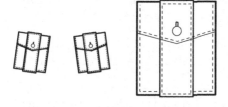

Box Pleat and Flap

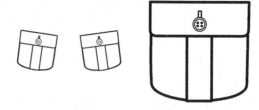

Box Pleat Center with Flap

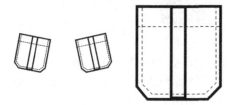

Box Pleat with Angled
Corners

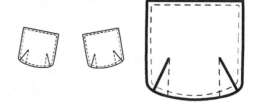

Corner Darts

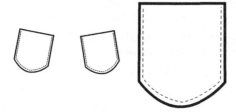

Curved Hemline

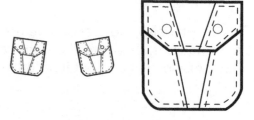

Design Lines with a
Flap and Topstitching

Patch Pockets

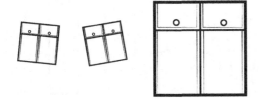

Double Patch with
Button Flap

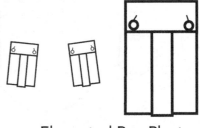

Elongated Box Pleat

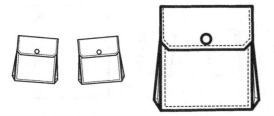

Gusseted (Bellowed)

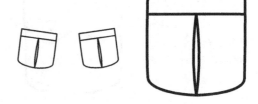

Inverted Pleat

Kangaroo Pouch

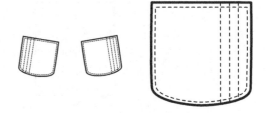

Pencil Side Pockets

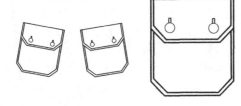

Piping along the Edges and Flap

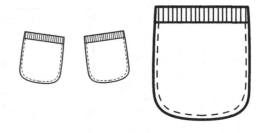

Rib Top

Rounded Corners

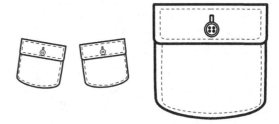

Rounded with Flap and Topstitching

Patch Pockets

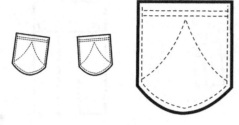

Rounded with Topstitching

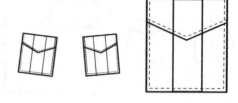

Safari Styling

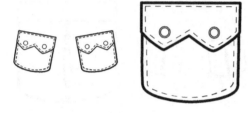

Sawtooth

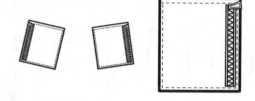

Square Corners and Side Zipper

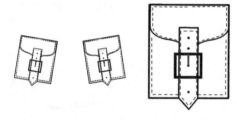

Strap Flap with Buckle Closure

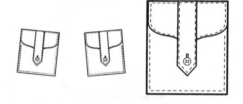

Strap Flap with Button Closure

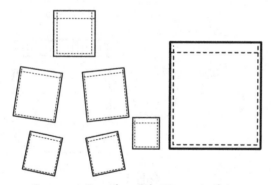

Square Patch with Topstitching

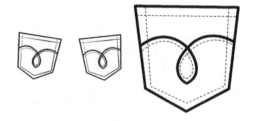

Traditional Jeans Topstitching

V-shape Topstitching

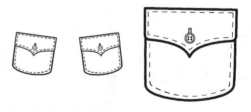

Western

Patch Pockets

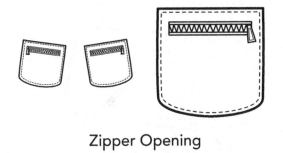

Zipper Opening

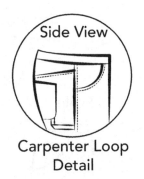

Side View

Carpenter Loop Detail

My Customized Patch Pockets

Front Pockets

Close Up

To Scale

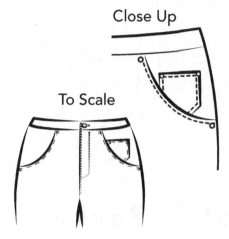

Coin
(Mini)

Curved Opening - Deep

Continental

Diagonal Clean Finished
(Slanted or Slashed)

Flapped Watch Pocket
(Fob Pocket)

Frogmouth

Front Pockets

Internal Pocket with Flap

L-shaped

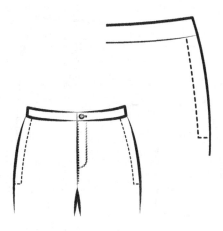

On-seam
(Vertical)

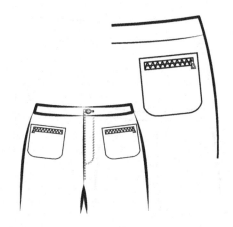

Patch with Zipper

Patch with Zippered Hand
Opening

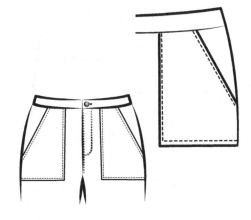

Rectangular Patch with a
Diagonal Opening

Pockets, Waistbands, and Other Design Details

Front Pockets

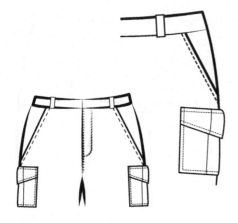

Side Patch Cargo

Single Welt with Button

Slanted (Diagonal or Slashed)

Smile

Sharp Curve

Traditional Curve with
Coin (Mini)

Front Pockets

Topstitched Kissing Welt

Zippered Coin Pocket

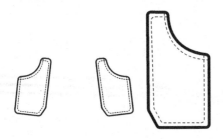

Front Hand Patch Plate with a
Single Topstitching

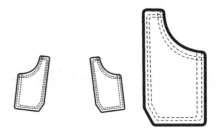

Front Hand Patch Plate with
Double Topstitching

My Customized Front Pockets

Welt Pockets and Pocket Flaps

Double Welt
(Jetted or Kissing Welt)

Double Welt - Curved with Reinforcement
(Western)

Double Welt with Opening Gap
and Single Topstitching

Double Welt with Reinforcement

Double Welt with Tab
(Jetted or Kissing Welt)

Double Welt with Topstitching
(Jetted or Kissing Welt)

Double Welt with Zipper
(Jetted or Kissing Welt)

Flap Welt Patched On

Single Welt
(Jetted or Besom when on
the Chest)

 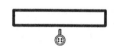

Single Welt with Button
(Jetted or Besom when on
the Chest)

Welt Pockets and Pocket Flaps

Singe Welt - Curved
(Barchetta or Besom when on the Chest)

Single Welt with Topstitching
(Jetted or Besom when on
the Chest)

Angled Corner Flap

Basic Flap

  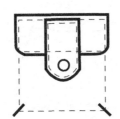

Single Topstitching and Tab on Flap

 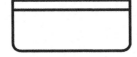

Welt with Flap (Jetted)

My Customized Welt Pockets and Pocket Flaps

Waistbands

Basic - Narrow

Basic - Wide

Drawstring

Elastic

Elastic - Exposed

Elastic - Side

Extended Center Front

Ruffled Elastic

Inner Facing along the Waistline

Inside View

This must have interfacing.

Straight
This is not curved or contoured.

Standard Jeans

Yoke Waistline (Wide)

V-shaped Yoke

Belts

Belt with a Square Buckle

Belt with a Round Buckle

Knotted Tie

Ribbon Tie

Wrapped Bow

Wrapped Knot

Beltloops, Buckles, and Trims

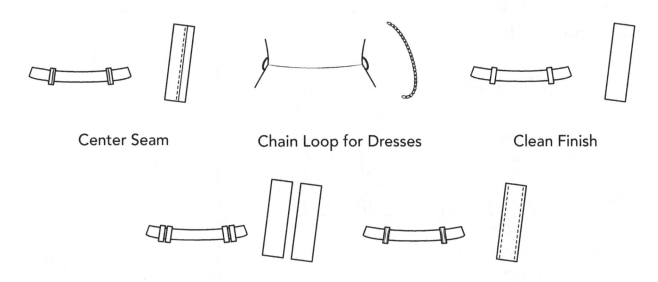

Center Seam

Chain Loop for Dresses

Clean Finish

Double

Standard with Topstitching

Buckles, Drawstrings, Rivets, and Topstitching

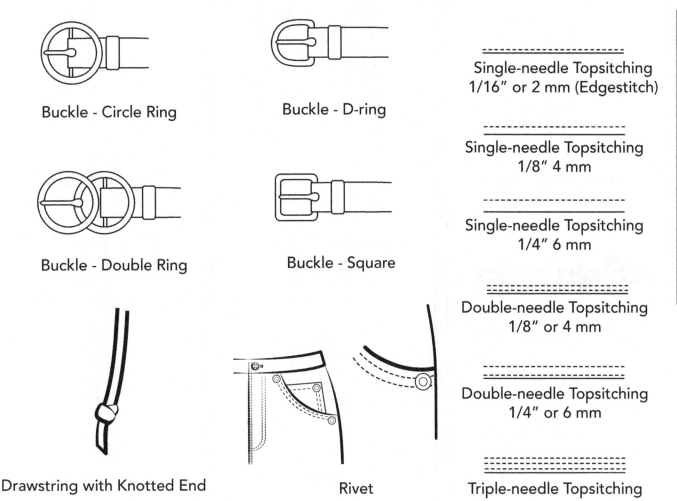

Buckle - Circle Ring

Buckle - D-ring

Single-needle Topsitching
1/16" or 2 mm (Edgestitch)

Single-needle Topsitching
1/8" 4 mm

Single-needle Topsitching
1/4" 6 mm

Buckle - Double Ring

Buckle - Square

Double-needle Topsitching
1/8" or 4 mm

Double-needle Topsitching
1/4" or 6 mm

Drawstring with Knotted End

Rivet

Triple-needle Topsitching

Closures

Buttonholes, Button Loops, and Buttons

Standard Buttonhole and 4-Hole Button

Keyhole Buttonhole and Shank Button

Button Loops and Shank Buttons

Chinese Knot and Frog

Lacing

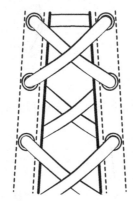

Eyelet

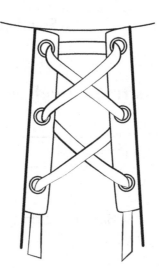

Grommet with Extended Flap

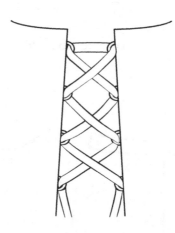

Loops

Zippers

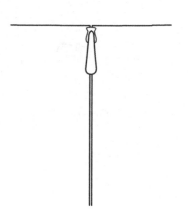

Invisible (Kissing)

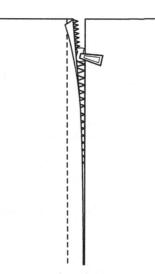

Single Placket

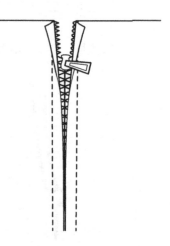

Kissing Placket

My Customized Waistbands, Belts, Beltloops, and Trims

My Customized Waistbands, Belts, Beltloops, and Trims

Faces, Hair, Hands, and Shoes

Generally, flat garment sketches do not include faces, hair, hands, and shoes. Fashion Flats are meant to be technical drawings and used for developing the product and merchandising the styles into complete collections.

However, I thought it would be fun to include some options in case you want a more 3-dimensional appearance that progresses toward a fashion illustration. Have fun selecting the look of your model. Modify the sketches to create a few look-alikes of yourself for your croquis library.

Scan this QR code to watch this free video to learn how to draw faces and hair:

Scan this QR code to view more videos in the exclusive FREE Video Vault:

Drawing Faces with Proportional Guidelines

Proportion of Facial Features:

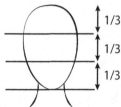

1. Draw a horizontal guideline at the bottom of the head. Then, add two guidelines a third of the total head height.

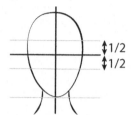

2. Draw a vertical guideline down the center of the head. Then, add one horizontal guideline splitting the middle horizontal section in half.

3. The eyebrows go slightly below the top guideline.

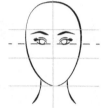

4. The bottom of the eyes rest on the center horizontal guideline.

5. The bottom of the nose goes below the lower horizontal guideline.

6. Cheekbone lines start slightly above the lower horizontal guideline. These are optional. Render the lines with tonal markers.

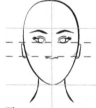

7. The ears go near the cheekbones between the lower two guidelines.

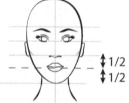

8. Add a guideline halfway between the lower horizontal guidelines. The center of the mouth goes on this guideline.

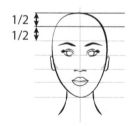

9. Add a guideline at the top of the head and halfway between the top two guidelines.

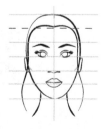

10. Draw the hairline at the guideline below the top of the head.

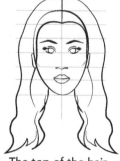

11. The top of the hair can have as much fullness as you wish. A starting point is approximately the same line distance as the other line spacing.

12. Erase the proportional guidelines, top head shape, and the ears behind the hair. Add pupils to the eyes.

Drawing Facial Features Step by Step

Steps for Drawing Eyes and Eyebrows:

Steps for Drawing the Nose and Mouth:

Face Shapes

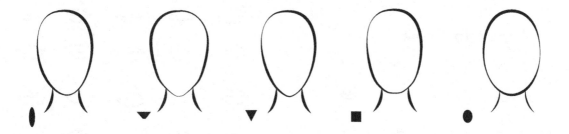

Face Shapes with Proportional Guidelines

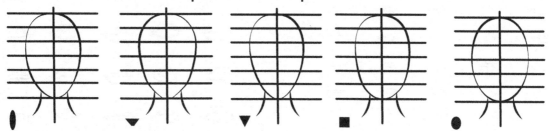

Facial Features

Eyebrows and Eyes - to Scale

Eyebrows and Eyes - Enlarged

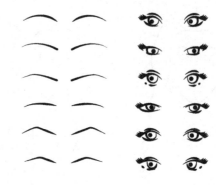

Noses - to Scale

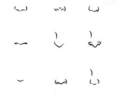

Noses - Enlarged

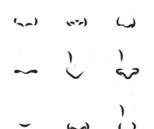

Ears - Enlarged

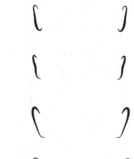

Ears - to Scale

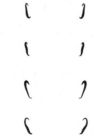

Lips - Enlarged

Lips - to Scale

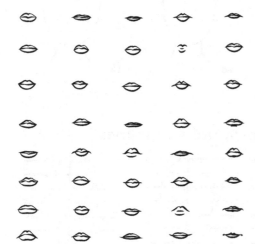

Hair

Hands and Shoes

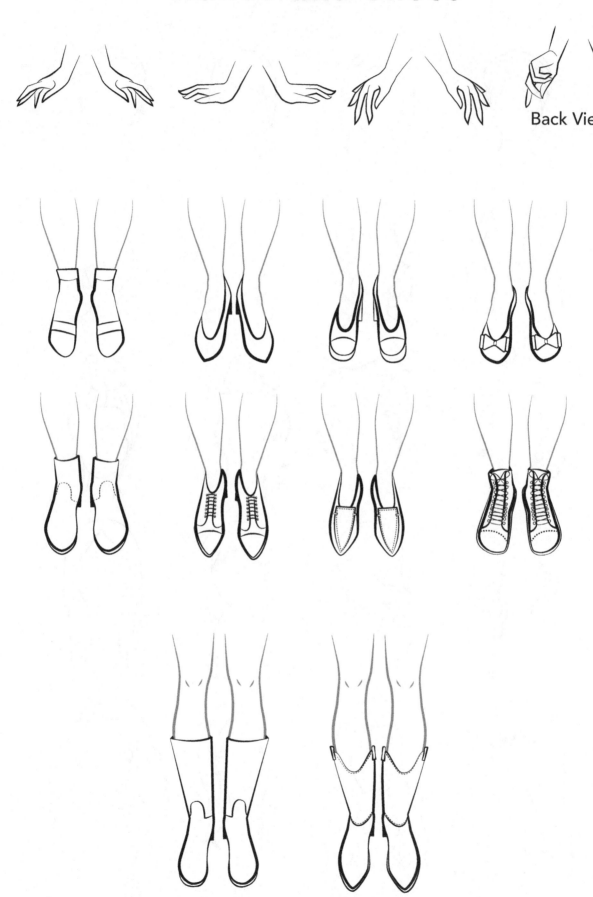

Back View

Drawing the Back View

Throughout this book, the primary view is the front. However, as a designer, you must also consider the back of the garment. I did not include back views in this library because they are straightforward to create. Doing this process without a direct sketch is an excellent test of your creativity.

To draw the back view of your garments, place a piece of tracing or marker paper over your front view. Trace the outside silhouette of your style. This outer silhouette line is the same on the front and back images.

Draw the back view with any design lines or style details you envision. Ensure that design lines from the front align with the back at the side areas. Look at garments in your collection to mimic any design details, and draw them.

Before cutting and sewing styles, drawing the back of the garment is important to help you analyze the entire design process. Once again, it's always easier to erase a few lines on a sketch than it is to adjust a garment after the fabric has been cut.

How do you create the back view? Scan this QR code to watch a free video and learn:

The Digital Fashion Design Book

Would you like to use the sketches in this book in Adobe® Illustrator® or in Procreate®?

Digital sketches are often used in professional portfolios and the garment industry for tech packs. An example of a flat garment sketch used within a tech pack is in the introduction of this book on page 14. This entire book was sketched in Adobe® Illustrator®.

If you have a subscription of Adobe® Illustrator®, you can digitally sketch your ideas with this vector-based program. With Adobe® Illustrator®, you can edit the sketches in this book by purchasing an editable version (.ai file type).

If you have the digital app Procreate®, you can purchase and use the digital file of the book (.pr file type) as a reference while sketching.

This book has no affiliation with Adobe® Illustrator® or Procreate®.

Scan this QR code to buy *The Fashion Design Book* as an editable digital book (.ai and .pr file types):

Scan this QR code to watch a free video that shows how to use *The Fashion Design Book* in Adobe® Illustrator®:

Scan this QR code to watch a free video about manual vs. digital drawing:

Scan this QR code to watch a free video that shows how to use *The Fashion Design Book* in Procreate®:

Acknowledgments

Thank you to all who have helped make this book a reality, especially my editors, Wayne and Dianne Vogt. You have both always been my mentors throughout my lifetime, and I am so thankful for you.

Thank you to all the artists who have helped create illustrations to make this a well-rounded collection: Sarah Marsh, Ariana Brolagda, Jazmin Perea, and Adantia Piliang.

Thank you to the video editors who have spent countless hours on multiple rounds of edits to get the quality up to my standard: Jhonmaren Calo and Tetiana Zhdanova.

Thank you, Shahadat A. Shakit, for all your effort in the layout and design and Svetlana Uscumlic for the cover design.

And finally, thank you, Luisa Silvestre, for helping with social media coordination and helping throughout the book creation process.

With all of your effort, this book came to fruition.

Conclusion

Congratulations! By now, you are well underway in designing your (or your clients') collections! I hope you have learned a lot about sketching and feel inspired to design beautiful clothes that are entirely your style.

If you want to take your skills to the next level, I highly recommend joining me for the online course "Define, Design, & Love Your Style." This very thorough course walks you through the many steps throughout the design process. It can be used for your collection or your clients' collections.

You will study silhouettes to understand what is flattering on specific body types (including yours). You will define your favorite colors, fabrics, silhouettes, and style details so that your entire collection reflects the look you want to portray.

This course will challenge you to merchandise your collection to ensure it is 100% your style. This is a fun and creative process, and it will strengthen your design sense.

All these design topics come together in the online course to create a style that represents your personality. You will have defined and designed a style you love. The goal is to create a cohesive collection and love every garment in your closet.

Scan this QR code to sign up to be notified for the next online course enrollment for Define, Design, & Love Your Style:

Thank you for joining me on this fun and creative journey. It has been an honor to guide you through the fashion design sketching process. Fashion is not just about following trends but also about expressing your unique personality and style. Never be afraid to experiment and try new things. Enjoy the journey of defining and designing your style.

Continue to pursue your dreams, and do not be discouraged by obstacles or setbacks. Often, these struggles push us to grow and learn in unexpected ways.

Watch this video to learn how goals and dreams may change over time:

You can achieve anything you set your mind to with passion, dedication, and perseverance. Keep sketching, designing, and creating the clothes of your dreams!

Meet Gina Renee

Gina Renee has been working in the garment industry since 2003, when she graduated from the Fashion Institute of Technology (FIT) in New York City (NYC). Directly after graduating with a fashion design degree, she worked in high fashion in NYC, fitting beautiful gowns and tailoring women's suits.

After living in NYC for five years, she moved to California where she worked for two leading action sports clothing brands, creating snowboarding outerwear and surfing boardshorts.

In 2012, Gina and her husband moved to Germany where she worked as a freelance patternmaker and started Gina Renee Designs, an Indie sewing pattern company. To view her sewing pattern collection and download her patterns, visit www.GinaReneeDesigns.com.

She has lived in Switzerland since 2014, where she led a talented team of patternmakers and developers at a well-known European sportswear brand. In 2022, she decided to go full-time with her business, teaching about patternmaking, fitting, and designing. With this, Gina has found her true calling by sharing all the information she learned while working in the garment industry.

Her main task while working in the garment industry has always been to develop quality clothes that fit well. She has fitted tens of thousands of garments during her career. Gina has fitted numerous top performing athletes from several different nations. Several have won gold medals in the world's highest international competitions while wearing garments she fitted for them. Gina has always loved the technical side of fitting, and her goal is to help you achieve the perfectly-fitting clothes you dream of.

She is also the creator of The GRD Method™ of patternmaking and designing. GRD stands for Gina's name. Her online course, "Making a Moulage – The GRD Method™," gives you a solid foundation in patternmaking from which you can design the clothes of your dreams. The online design course "Define, Design, & Love Your Style – The GRD Method™" teaches you how to create an entire collection that flatters your body type. The course "Mastering Garment Ease – The GRD Method™" shows you how to execute pattern corrections before cutting a fitting sample so that you have fewer fitting frustrations.

More information can be found at www.GRDMethod.com or at www.GinaRenee.com.

Gina grew up in Colorado and is a nature-girl by heart. She is happy to be living near nature once again in Switzerland. During her free time, she enjoys hiking, swimming, and cycling in the beautiful Swiss Alps. And let's not forget her most important hobby – sewing!

Made in the USA
Las Vegas, NV
03 June 2024

90626170R00096